Praise for the First Edition

"I am awed at the accomplishments of this truly great scholar, indeed the greatest American Italianist of the 20th century. It is a very beautiful book, very elegantly done … [It] gave me some truly memorable moments of reading and contemplation."

– Enikö Bollobás (Associate Professor and Chair,
Department of American Studies, Eötvös Loránd University, Budapest, Hungary)

"A splendid tribute to the memory of a scholar I admired very much for her originality and finesse of interpretations."

– Paolo Cherchi (Professor Emeritus of Italian and Spanish Literatures,
University of Chicago)

"A wonderful list and tribute. Especially I liked the love story, and this book as one new chapter in the story."

–Donald Wesling (Professor Emeritus of English Literature,
University of California, San Diego)

"It is nice to see a catalogue that takes account not only of the scholarly production of a writer but also the physical form in which each publication appeared. … A service to book history and Dante studies both."

– Paul F. Gehl (Custodian of the John M. Wing Foundation
on the History of Printing, The Newberry Library, Chicago, Illinois)

"The Catalogue is an important and beautiful publication."

– Marylène Altieri (Curator of Printed Books, Schlesinger Library,
Radcliffe Institute for Advanced Study, Harvard University

"A lovely, loving and worthy tribute."

– H. Wayne Storey (Professor of Italian,
Director of the Medieval Studies Institute, Indiana University, Bloomington)

"Here we have glimpses of depth and width—real rubrics of texts to be cherished in full elsewhere. It is so unexpected to have such beauty and elegance in the genre."

– Raimo Anttila (Professor Emeritus of Linguistics and Indo-European Studies,
University of California, Los Angeles)

"The photograph of Marianne is a gem: it captures both her beauty and her poignant earnestness as a survivor of a personal history that was marked by repeated injustices which tested her morale but did not overcome her will to find and express the highest meanings that poetry can attain. . . . She was like a virtuoso musician who has mastered her instrument as a medium of artistic interpretation. . . . Marianne left us a wonderful legacy of poetic truth for which we can all be grateful."

– Eugene Vance (Emeritus Professor of French, Comparative Literature and
Comparative Religion, University of Washington)

Donum redactoris —

January 6, 2013

MARIANNE SHAPIRO

A CATALOGUE RAISONNÉ

OF

HER PUBLICATIONS

Second Edition

With Tributes by
Robert Hatten and Claudia Moscovici

Compiled and Edited
by
Michael Shapiro

2010

MARIANNE SHAPIRO
A CATALOGUE RAISONNÉ OF HER PUBLICATIONS

Copyright © by Michael Shapiro, 2009. All rights reserved. Printed in the United States of America.

Shapiro, Michael, 1939-
  Marianne Shapiro
  A Catalogue Raisonné of Her Publications.
 p. cm.

Photograph of Marianne Shapiro
by Constance Brown (Providence, R. I.)

Reprinted by permission:
  The University of Chicago Press [review of
  Hieroglyph of Time: The Petrarchan Sestina]
  EBS Service for Publishers, Lucerne
  (Switzerland), *The Unknown Leonardo*
  ["The Words of Leonardo"]
  Review of Marianne Shapiro's *De vulgari
  eloquentia: Dante's Book of Exile*, from volume
  3, number 2, pp. 478-485 of *Envoi: A Review
  Journal of Medieval Literature*, 1997.
  Copyright 1994 AMS Press, Inc.
  All rights reserved.

Second Edition, 2010,
Scotts Valley, Calif.
ISBN 1453895469

Front cover: drawing by Botticelli for Par. XXX
Back cover: drawing by Botticelli for Par. XXVIII

Book design by Carol Pentleton

To our meeting in the Empyrean,
and to our Gebu with love

Se quanto infino a qui di lei si dice
fosse conchiuso tutto in una loda,
poca sarebbe a fornir questa vice.
La bellezza ch'io vidi si trasmoda
non pur di là da noi, ma certo io credo
che solo il suo fattor tutta la goda.
Da questo passo vinto mi concedo
più che già mai da punto di suo tema
soprato fosse comico o tragedo:
ché, come sole in viso che più trema,
così lo rimembrar del dolce riso
la mente mia da me medesmo scema.
Dal primo giorno ch'i' vidi il suo viso
in questa vita, infino a questa vista,
non m'è il seguire al mio cantar preciso;
ma or convien che mio seguir desista
più dietro a sua bellezza, poetando,
come a l'ultimo suo ciascuno artista.

Dante, Par. XXX.16-33

TABLE OF CONTENTS

APPENDICES

Compiler's Note to the Second Edition

The original idea for this Second Edition arose in conjunction with an Exhibit of the Books of Marianne Shapiro, which was to be mounted in October 2010 at her alma mater, the Fiorello H. LaGuardia High School of Music & Art and Performing Arts in Manhattan. The two tributes by Robert Hatten and Claudia Moscovici reproduced here were to be delivered at the Opening of the Exhibit. Sadly, however, this project did not come to fruition. Instead, a special exhibit, "The Life and Work of Marianne Shapiro," can be viewed online (www.marianneandmichaelshapiro.com).

I am profoundly grateful to all the readers of the first edition whose generous responses gave added impetus to the creation of this second edition. Most of all I am grateful to Robert Hatten and Claudia Moscovici for their moving tributes. These encomia testify to their subject's enduring stature and assuage my unending grief.

Michael Shapiro
Manchester Center, Vermont
October 2010

A Tribute to Marianne and Michael

Robert Hatten
(Professor of Music Theory, Jacobs School of Music,
Indiana University, Bloomington)

Because my memories of Marianne are always of Marianne with Michael, this tribute is really to their memorable love for each other. I recall meeting them at Semiotic Society conferences, where her warmth and his responsiveness were immediately evident, along with a mind that could find connections between dance, Peirce's categories, and the Trinity! What a remarkable couple, I thought, when reading their joint and interleaving essays on style in language. Two of their collaborations, on the life cycle of a trope, and the status of irony—were special favorites. I had met Michael as a result of researching my dissertation on style in music and my first book on musical meaning in Beethoven. I had read Michael's important book on asymmetry in poetry and later consulted with him on the concept of markedness, driving up from Penn (where I was on a fellowship in 1985-86) to meet with him over dinner at Princeton. Through Michael I had the opportunity to get to know Marianne better, and the highlight was a visit to their beautiful apartment in New York, where I heard Marianne play on her Steinway grand with such soulfulness and beauty of sound that I realized she could have made her career as a musician. Again, the warmth and generosity of her person left the deepest impression, despite a scintillating conversation ranging among the arts and ideas.

Now, through Michael's continued responsiveness in disseminating her legacy, I have been encountering Marianne's splendid investigations into the poetic works of Dante and Petrarch. Her *Hieroglyph of Time* has been a revelation, given my own interest in the sestina. I absorbed Marianne's interpretations of Petrarch and the genre in order to guide my composition of a memorial sestina (see below), in which Petrarch's themes would be wedded to Marianne's life and work, but also to Michael's deeply felt love, through which, like Dante, he suffered such grief over the untimely death of his beloved. For in his own glowing memorial to Marianne's life and work, Michael has in effect created a *Vita Nuova* for the new century that draws forth the light of his Beatrice, immortalizing the miracles of their love, their communion of ideas, and her special brilliance as scholar and creative writer. In his quest, Michael has drawn on resources not available to Dante, whose loss came so much sooner, and whose poetic language could but create a divine abstraction in place of the woman he never had a chance to know as well. Michael was more fortunate, and through his efforts we are also fortunate to come to know Marianne as a vital presence, a fully realized individual, and an intellect who left the world a body of work that has yet to be fully assimilated by scholars or appreciated by readers. Through Michael's testimony of their conversational exchanges, captured in his elegant recreation of the earliest genre of the Japanese novel, we can experience the reality (not mere fiction, as the companion volume attests—and as Dante would approve, given his own commentaries on the autobiographical inspirations for his poems) of their extraordinary intellectual life. Through Michael's monument to her work, we can begin to discover the depth of her artistic vision, and begin to appreciate how in transcending academic pettiness and betrayal she achieved more than many a tenured professor in her field: a model critical practice in which a theoretical synthesis of sound and meaning supports an historically contextualized interpretation of a living poetic tradition.

In offering the following poem, then, I hope to exemplify one way in which Marianne's influential legacy as artist and scholar continues to thrive, linking us to one of the great sources of vernacular poetry. Also, to offer, as a sympathetic friend, an acknowledgement of Michael's great love, as witnessed by the profundity of his grief and the emergence of his own *Vita Nuova*.

May 31, 2010

Sestina for Michael and Marianne

(In memoriam, Marianne Shapiro)

When she wrote of time's inexorable march
Through the sestinas of Petrarch, their echoes of
death,
Impossible ends transfigured by true love,
Or the constancy of a lover, alone or bereft—
It was as though she sensed the lineage of her life
In the form, the measured lines, the web of signs,

And recoiled, as the permutation of six end-signs
Marked the cadence of a hopeless march,
Or the unraveling spiral of a life,
Its coded sequence of genes. But untimely death
Would leave one devoid of allegory. Bereft
Of her voice, its gestures of dialogic love,

He would ache for reassurance, evidence that love
Could penetrate the necropolis of signs,
Unlock the cipher of a blank slab bereft
Of meaning: the victimizing, persecuting march
Of cells gone mad, the cruel regime of Death. . . .
He grieved the more, the more he felt her life
Spilling over the dark edge, a phantom life
Of fervid dreams dispelled by tears. Through love
He'd seek to diminish all-consuming death
As but the frame foregrounding a flow of signs,
But wavering at that threshold, his inward march
Betrayed him at a loss. Though still bereft

Of her presence, he struggled not to be reft
Of what remained, what might become of life:
As April supersedes a wintry March,
Her heaven-sent, his ever-present love
Might consummate a bond beyond all signs'
Endearing, enduring thus her cruel death . . .

Leave off, reject that attitude toward death!
Bereave, but then release, be not bereft:
You hold within your emptiness the signs
That can restore, that will break through to life.
Loosen up the desperate knot of love;
Admit a softer 'twining. No raging march

Unto the dismal border-march of death!
She would not leave this world a love bereft:
For all who read her life renew her signs.

Robert Hatten
Nov. 15-23, 2009

Marianne Shapiro: Mentor, Friend, and Renaissance Woman

Claudia Moscovici (Notablewriters.com)

I met Professor Marianne Shapiro in my second year of graduate studies in Comparative Literature at Brown University. I recall how she immediately created a uniquely positive impression on me and other students. From the start, she struck me as friendly and personable, exuding an aura of great cultural range and sophistication along with a sense of natural charm and modesty. It was obvious that she was well versed not only in the writings of the Italian Renaissance, her field of specialization, but also in Shakespeare, eighteenth and nineteenth-century French literature, art and… the lost art of conversation.

By the time I met Marianne I had taken graduate courses in Comparative Literature and Cultural Studies for over a year. I had already been exposed to feminist, poststructuralist, postmodernist and postcolonial theories: which is to say, like every Comp. Lit. student of my generation at Brown University, to just about every "post" that was popular at the time. What seemed to be noticeably lacking from some of my courses, however, was the reason why I wanted to study the literature in the first place: a love of the novels themselves; a love of understanding their cultural contexts and of speaking and writing as clearly as possible about them; to share that love of knowledge with others. It seemed that this love of literature was perceived, at the time, as a thing of the past: a cultural relic of humanistic studies that had been rendered nearly obsolete by newer and more sophisticated cultural theories. Reading Derrida's deconstruction of Rousseau was seen by many in Cultural Studies as more informative and interesting than reading Rousseau himself.

If Marianne Shapiro stood out in that academic context it was because she seemed to have a deep knowledge and appreciation of the original literature and culture that she shared with us. She also had a conversational manner of interacting with students that made the material we studied together seem all the more engaging. She spoke clearly, involved us in intellectual conversations, and focused on our individual strengths and interests, so that each student could benefit as much as possible from her course. She never imposed upon us any particular theory or way of thought, although it was very clear that she, herself, was well versed in literary theories, from semiotics, to structuralism and post-structuralism. Yet for her, as for many of us, the love of literature seemed primary, and the theories she applied to texts became a way of understanding them better: of underscoring some of their narrative strategies and features that would help us appreciate them on a deeper level.

As a mentor, teacher, and friend, Marianne was very nurturing to her students. Her style wasn't so much maternal, however, as that of what you'd expect a woman of great culture to be like: confident enough of her expertise to be encouraging rather than overbearing and flexible rather than prescriptive. In my eyes, she was like a modern-day *salonnière* or, to use a term more appropriate for her area of specialization, a modern day Renaissance woman: knowledgeable about so many fields, talented in so many genres and able to convey that breadth of culture not just through her scholarship but also through her style of being, through her communication skills, and through her versatility as a writer in several genres.

Given everything I knew about her, I was not surprised when I found out from her husband, Michael Shapiro, that Marianne has published a novel about the ivory tower, called *Higher Learning*, which received very high praise from fellow scholars and literary critics. I read her novel with great pleasure and found it not only extremely entertaining—filled with irony and humor—but also right on the mark about happenings in academia which I had witnessed myself. *Higher Learning* is a slice of life, a testament of the politics of many fields in the arts and humanities in academia, similar in genre and style to David Lodge's *Small World*. Yet I found Marianne's novel even more daring and honest about the context it described. To offer one example: "The time and place were therefore just right for the deification of Palter Van Geyst and 'theory'. This strategy alone licensed people to do nothing and STILL PRETEND THEY WERE DOING SOME-THING. You could read not at all if you knew the right words to pronounce over books. The verbal gadgetry and mechanical moves of 'theory' were even getting media attention for the first time ever—real celebrity! SO WHO NEEDED THE BOOKS? Other professors." (*Higher Learning*, 79)

By way of contrast to many other professors, Marianne was a genuine lover of fiction and poetry. This was evident in the clear, informative, and loving way she talked about Shakespeare, about Dante, about Flaubert. It was partly due to the fact that she showed by personal example it was still possible to love novels, not just the theories about them, that I also followed a similar path and became a literary critic and fiction writer. Marianne Shapiro exuded a passion for culture that will be perpetuated by her students and that remains alive through her personal and intellectual legacy.

Introduction

This *Catalogue* provides a synoptic view of the scholarship of Marianne Shapiro (1940-2003), demonstrably the most accomplished and versatile American Italianist of the twentieth century. As a comparatist, medievalist, Dantist, and Renaissance specialist, her scope was unparalleled. While she was alive and still far from her peak as a scholar, it was already remarked of Marianne Shapiro by a fellow critic of the first rank that for intelligence, intellectual imagination, and productivity she had no peers in the field of Romance philology; and that to find her equals one would have to turn to such giants of two generations ago as Leo Spitzer and Erich Auerbach.

In this light, her characteristically unassuming self-assessment, written two years before her death, is worth reproducing here:

> "I have always been and continue to be involved in research and teaching in my original areas of specialization, the works of Dante and renaissance epic (Ariosto and Tasso), and my current research has broadened and deepened into an involvement with cultural studies. I have consistently brought an interdisciplinary perspective to teaching and writing, as well as a strong belief in practical criticism and in the importance of versatility.

"My first book, *Woman Earthly and Divine in the Comedy of Dante*, was also the first modern work on the poem's female characters as such. I continued this line of research by publishing the first American study of the female troubadours of the 12th century, which stimulated a considerable body of research. These publications, predating the feminist wave in the United States, have recently enjoyed a surge of renewed interest. The book I published in 1990, *De vulgari eloquentia, Dante's Book of Exile*, contains the only English translation of the treatise based on original scholarship and is routinely cited as a source of information and explication of Dante's language theory. I have also made permanent contributions to the store of general knowledge of the *Comedy* in a number of my forty-odd articles on the subject. My latest book, *Dante and the Knot of Body and Soul* (St. Martin's Press, 1998) will, I believe, open entirely new vistas for Dante studies.

"The scholarship summarized on my vita involves poetics and mythology as well as literary history. Over time it has drawn nearer to the concerns of Latinists and teachers of classics. *The Poetics of Ariosto*, for example, examines renaissance rewritings of mythological narratives, and the Dante research reevaluates the crucial structural impact of the *Aeneid* on the *Comedy* in a consistently analytical perspective. I try to stay clear of the twin pitfalls of literature being either self-referential or solely a cultural document.

"I have worked across disciplinary boundaries on such apparently disparate topics as ballet and television (the situation comedy *All in the Family*). *Figuration in Verbal Art* contains some of those pieces. In sum, they seek to establish a common interpretative language by which to examine the production of different arts within one compass.

"My current project is a book called *Constructing Leonardo*, based on a course I gave at Brown in 1991. It will study the cultural image of Leonardo da Vinci (man and work) as it has been fashioned and elaborated from his lifetime to the present day. Leonardo's own writings will figure among the data. Of special relevance will be an exploration of the relationship between art and science, including a section on the spiroform "hand" of Leonardo the draftsman. Most of the book will deal with the Leonardo "myth" (including androgyny) built up over centuries and composed of a mélange of legend, art history, Freudian diagnosis, fictional reconstruction, modernist manifesto, and popular culture including film (such as *Mona Lisa*).

"My distinguishing trait as a teacher is versatility. I have wide experience of and a deep attachment to teaching at every level, and I hope to continue exploring new areas of research and offering courses aimed at a variety of student audiences, including undergraduates with little university experience in humanistic studies. Two of the Ph.D.s whose doctoral dissertations I directed had little or no acquaintance with Italian literature or Provençal when they became my students; I saw them through their entire course of study. At the other end of the spectrum, it has been especially satisfying to watch the progress of language students, all the more so because English, not Italian, was my first language, and my approach benefits from an experience analogous to theirs. An ability to adjust to changing circumstances is, I believe, essential to success in teaching, as is a problem-solving attitude."

From Appendix A of this *Catalogue* it will transpire—to those who are not already aware of her professional history—that Marianne managed to persevere in accomplishing the research and writing represented here despite being compelled to migrate for thirty-five years between sundry universities, deprived over the entirety of her career of the permanent position she so richly deserved and that was routinely afforded scholars of lesser stature. Those who insouciantly claim that the life of what is now called an "independent scholar"—a misnomer if ever there was one, as Marianne wittily remarked, such persons in fact being *acutely* "dependent"—conduces to greater productivity by freeing up time that would otherwise be consumed by classroom teaching and all the quotidian tasks of a modern professorial career, are simply committing the error born of inexperience. Nothing is in fact more daunting to an aspiring scholar than the denial of recognition and acceptance that comes as a result of being ceaselessly shunted to the periphery of academic life. For a woman, in particular, to overcome the utterly unjust obstacles that were forever being placed in Marianne's career path is especially difficult, and it is a monumental tribute to the strength of her intellectual commitment that she succeeded in creating a superlative scholarly legacy despite these impediments.

Until the illness leading to her death made it impossible to continue her research and writing, Marianne had plans for several future books, one of which was on Leonardo (outlined in Appendix C). A second was a book on leadership for corporate executives based on her own strikingly original analysis of the *Aeneid*, especially of Aeneas himself. Finally, there was a germinating plan for a book on Italian moral philosophy in the sixteenth century. The last manuscript that Marianne actually worked on herself but left unfinished was "Rereading Dostoevskij's *Dvojnik*," which was completed by me and prepared for publication in the journal *Russian Literature*.

In compiling and publishing this *Catalogue* it has been my intention to honor the memory of a uniquely talented scholar by giving a full account of her publications. I am, moreover, convinced that when the educational blinders preventing students of medieval Italian literature — Dante in particular — from distinguishing the gold from the dross in extant criticism have been removed by the passage of time and by the concomitant death of malign prejudices, it is the publications of Marianne Shapiro that will forever remain a powerful inspiration and an endless source of discovery for future generations of scholars and readers.

M. S.
Los Angeles, Calif.

I. BOOKS AND MONOGRAPHS

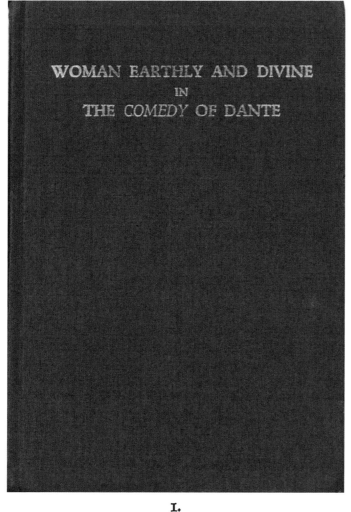

I.

WOMAN EARTHLY AND DIVINE IN THE COMEDY OF DANTE. STUDIES IN ROMANCE LANGUAGES, VOLUME 12. 187 PP. LEXINGTON: UNIVERSITY PRESS OF KENTUCKY, 1975.

Casebound in red bookcloth with gold foil stamping; 6.45"x9.125"

CONTENTS

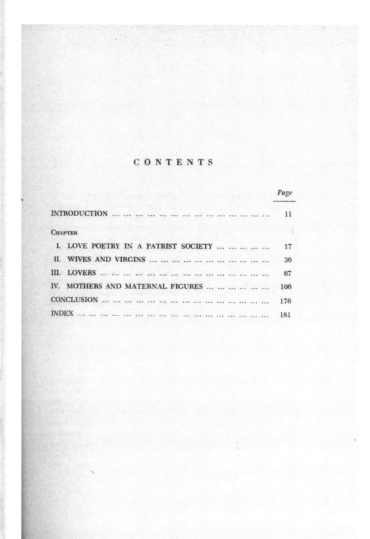

This book started life as a doctoral dissertation in the Department of Italian at Columbia University. In the Butler Library catalog, there is the following entry:

Author: Shapiro, Marianne Goldner, 1940-
Title: *Woman, earthly and divine, in the Comedy of Dante.*
Publisher/Date: New York 1968.

Marianne's dissertation adviser was John Charles Nelson, the senior Dantist in the Department at the time. When she presented what she thought would be the final draft of her work to Nelson, it ran to more than 500 double-spaced pages, including a wealth of historical and culturological material—the fruit of much independent research and thought—to support her comprehensive analysis of the *Comedy's* women characters. Unfortunately, Nelson insisted that she cut much of this valuable material from the final version. Because this work of excision coincided with a particularly fraught period (1969-1972) of her professional life, Marianne chose not to reconstitute the original uncut version for publication, for which she was criticized in at least one review of the book.

But the following testimonial twenty-five years after the book's appearance—from one of the world's leading scholars of the history of Christianity and medieval intellectual history—will surely stand the test of time:

> "Of the vast literature in the field, including the several series of Lectura Dantis and standard works of reference, I have read more than I have used here, and used more than I have cited here. But for their special contributions to my understanding of many specific issues, there are two books in my bibliography to which I want to call attention (as it happens, the first is by a former [Yale] colleague and the second by a former student): Marianne Shapiro, *Woman Earthly and Divine in the "Comedy" of Dante*, and Barbara Newman, *Sister of Wisdom: St. Hildegard's Theology of the Feminine*."
>
> – Jaroslav Pelikan, in the Preface to his *Eternal Feminines: The Three Theological Allegories in Dante's Paradiso* (1990)

Studies
in
Semiotics

Hierarchy and
the Structure of
Tropes

Michael and Marianne
Shapiro

Research Center for Language and Semiotic Studies
(Indiana University) with The Peter de Ridder Press

Saddlestitched;
6.0"x 9.0"

2.
HIERARCHY AND THE STRUCTURE OF TROPES
[COAUTHOR, MICHAEL SHAPIRO].
STUDIES IN SEMIOTICS, VOLUME 8. PP. V, 37.
BLOOMINGTON: INDIANA UNIVERSITY, 1976.

Table of Contents

A revised version of this monograph appeared as chapter 2 of *Figuration in Verbal Art* [see page 25].

TORONTO SEMIOTIC CIRCLE

Monographs, Working Papers and Prepublications

MARIANNE and MICHAEL SHAPIRO

STRUCTURE AND CONTENT:

ESSAYS IN APPLIED SEMIOTICS

VICTORIA UNIVERSITY, TORONTO M5S 1K7

1979, Number 2

Sidestitched;
8.5"x11.0"

3.
STRUCTURE AND CONTENT:
ESSAYS IN APPLIED SEMIOTICS
[COAUTHOR, MICHAEL SHAPIRO].
MONOGRAPHS, WORKING PAPERS AND
PREPUBLICATIONS OF THE TORONTO
SEMIOTIC CIRCLE,
1979/No. 2. 69 PP.
TORONTO:
VICTORIA UNIVERSITY, 1979.

Michael Shapiro
Dept. of Slavic Languages
University of California
Los Angeles

This is a photo-offset edition of essays that include printed versions of public lectures delivered by both authors before the Toronto Semiotic Circle in October, 1979.

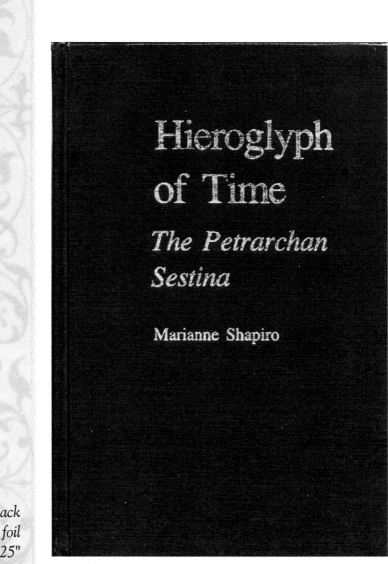

Casebound in black bookcloth with silver foil stamping; 6.125"x9.25"

4.
*HIEROGLYPH OF TIME:
THE PETRARCHAN SESTINA.
PP. XII, 254. MINNEAPOLIS:
UNIVERSITY OF MINNESOTA PRESS, 1980.*

Contents

vii

Marianne always considered this to be her best book. One review in particular tends to bear out her self-assessment:

"Marianne Shapiro's book on the Petrarchan sestina has eight chapters, moving from preliminary perspective-setting (chap. 1) through the development of the sestina form from Arnaut Daniel and Dante to its supreme use in Petrarch, through French, English, German, and Italian practitioners (chaps. 2-7), and ending with a highly compressed, theoretical five-page epilogue (chap. 8). Petrarch's *Le Rime* has as many poems as days in the year, but only nine of these are sestinas or double

sestinas, making a Petrarchan body of text for analysis of less than 400 lines. To the six sestinas by Petrarch she analyzes at length, Shapiro adds readings of sestinas by Arnaut, Guilhem de Saint-Grigori, Dante, Michelangelo, Pontus de Tyard, Sidney, Spenser, Pound, Ungaretti, Auden, Merwin, and Ashbery. She quotes the whole poem, gives a clear prose translation for work in languages other than English, and then patiently reads for structures of sound and sense, and for historical affiliation along the line of the sestina considered as a genre. (It is a genre, properly speaking, because it is not only thirty-nine lines with a certain fiendishly intricate disposition of end-words, but also a precisely imitable way of trapping time, a set of recurring amiable themes, a form of thought or family lan-

16

guage.) These many close readings bring the book's reader as near as may be to the ground level of poetic language, but they are so managed within the book's speculative structure that they constitute evidences for an over-arching theory of poetic language and of poetic influence.

"The many beautiful analyses have their special power by virtue of addressing simultaneously the formal and the semantic strata of the texts, as well as the placement of texts within the historical-philosophical series from Arnaut Daniel to Ashbery. The sestina form has its own inalienable imperatives, cruelly strict, but it is also susceptible to direction by aesthetic premises as different as Renaissance Platonism (Pontus de Tyard) and postmodern Derridianism (Ashbery). The book does show convincingly the greatness of Petrarch and shows how and why this is a late Medieval greatness. But while the Petrarchan sestina is in no sense a pretext, it stands here really as a massive test case for an inquiry into the language and history of the lyric in the West. It is the nature and handling of these larger concerns which lifts the book from the sole ownership of students of Petrarch, Italian literature, and poetic technique, making it a contribution to general poetics.

"Shapiro's merit is in her relating of poems to widening rings of context, from formal to philosophical to historical – and back. In passing, there is a range of mediating figures, from Plato and Pico della Mirandola to Heidegger and Hjelmslev. But throughout and centrally she pursues the aim stated in the first sentence of the first chapter, 'to reconcile the languages of literary scholarship . . . , synchronic analysis and historical criticism' (p. 3). Her intention for doing this is most openly declared in the highly compressed epilogue, where she challenges the antireferential and synchronic bias of much existing literary theory. Shapiro revises a set of terms taken from linguists, from Saussure by way of Hjelmslev, in order to show explicitly 'the fundamentally dynamic and unidirectional relation between content-form and expression-form that gives direction to poetry' (p. 238). The point (p. 237) is that 'language encompasses the content-substance of all other human sign systems,' including the second-order sign system which is poetic form.

"A sestina can and often does create its own tropes, turn its forms into a kind of content, but this 'expression-substance' is determined by a given poem's meanings, which have logical priority. The relations of content-substance and expression-substance, and of content-form and expression-form, are thus 'asymmetric, unidirectional, and transitive' (p. 237). If we understand this rightly, it is a wide generalizing of the claims of Michael Shapiro's inquiry into the linguistic structure of poetry, *Asymmetry* (1976), whose study of rhyme looked more narrowly at marked and unmarked features of language. Marianne Shapiro is making asymmetry into the crucial feature of poetic language and of the history of poetic influence. In this her book seems to challenge the poetics of Roman Jakobson, who has tended to prefer synchronic thinking and who has written influential studies on parallelism and structural symmetry.

"Without judging the ultimate merit of Shapiro's defense of asymmetry over symmetry as the poetic function par excellence, it must be said that this working hypothesis enables her to reveal many powerfully significant facts about her chosen poetic tradition. The sestina's main feature is rhyme on the same end-word in a different sentence and a different position. Same word in new position equals different meaning, necessarily. Contiguity and nonsynonymy of terms become structuring principles in sestinas that must rhyme by repetition, and these are principles of asymmetry of elements.

"Also examples of asymmetry are those famous impossibility figures in the Petrarchan rhetoric, oxymoron and adynaton, the latter receiving an especially brilliant reading in Shapiro's analyses. Further, in the introduction and in a whole chapter (chap. 3) on concepts of time, she shows how the Petrarchan sestina both forms its tropes and makes a religious argument when it dramatizes the meeting of cyclic and linear time, making thereby 'a model of meditation on poetic recurrence' (p. 18): 'Cyclical movement and movement that is directed toward a formal end contend with one another . . . so that the formal dismissal in the tornada [three-line final stanza] nevertheless betrays an open-ended doubt ...' (p. 19). Thus, through Petrarch's own self-division, can one of the most fiercely closed forms in the history of poetry beat back against itself. The sense of the sestina as genre, throughout its history, is that it is a 'knot of will and desire, closure and openness' (p. 27). The principle is at work also in poetic transmission, as Shapiro reveals through an account of the dialectics of Renaissance imitation in the case of Pontus de Tyard, member of the Pleiade and bishop of Chalon-Sur-Saone. Working with Petrarchan codes, this French imitator 'acted as the taxonomist of a landscape of recognition,' but at the same time as one who 'deranged this hierarchy' of systems of signification (p. 144).

"Of many other elements worthy of notice, we would single out Shapiro's treatment of concepts of time, her tracing of a line of pastoral sestina from Sidney through to Ashbery, and her systematic effort to keep sound and sense within a single thought.

"Shapiro has written a superlative book which will influence for decades to come the way we think about poetic technique. . . . it is on the basis of work of this order that prosody will perhaps, by century's end, find its true home within the human sciences."

— Donald Wesling and Enikö Bollobás, in *Modern Philology* 81:1 (1983)

Perfect binding

HIEROGLYPH OF TIME

THE PETRARCHAN SESTINA

Marianne Shapiro

The University of Minnesota Press has included this book as a print-on-demand title in its Minnesota Archive Editions program. The image shown above is of this paperback edition.

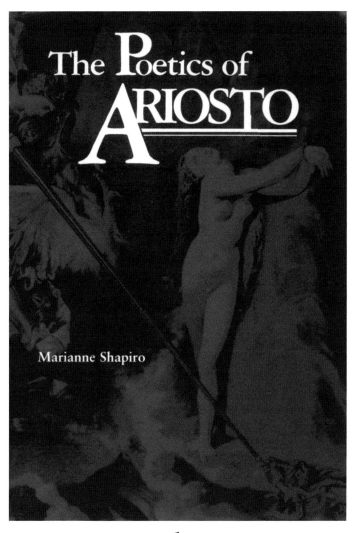

The Poetics of ARIOSTO

Marianne Shapiro

Casebound in blue bookcloth with silver foil stamping on the spine; offset lithograph dustjacket; 6.125"x9.25"

5.
THE POETICS OF ARIOSTO.
278 PP. DETROIT:
WAYNE STATE UNIVERSITY PRESS, 1988.

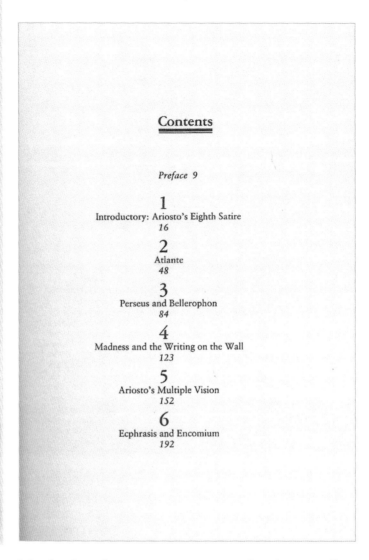

Contents

Preface 9

The startling originality of this book is, for reasons unconnected with its intellectual force but with the sociology of knowledge, hardly reflected in reviews, but cf. the following encomium:

> "Shapiro's notion of deconstruction . . . privileges poetic discourse over critical discourse, notes influences and precursors, searches for bridges between the satires and the poem, and identifies what it judges are adequate constitutive symbols of the poem's activity. High-Church 'deconstructionism' would probably condemn her methodology as heterodox. Nevertheless, this does not detract from either the validity of her enterprise or the value of her conclusions. The following mélange and dia-

logue should offer some sense of both the richness of her perceptions and their originality.

"Her chapter on the madness of Orlando observes the high standard of perceptiveness and clarity she maintains throughout.

"This study . . . remains among the most useful, challenging and innovative to appear in recent years. She has brought to the *Orlando furioso* the same wide-ranging erudition and sensitivity that has distinguished her work on the *Divine Comedy*."

— James T. Chiampi, in *Italica* 67:4 (1990)

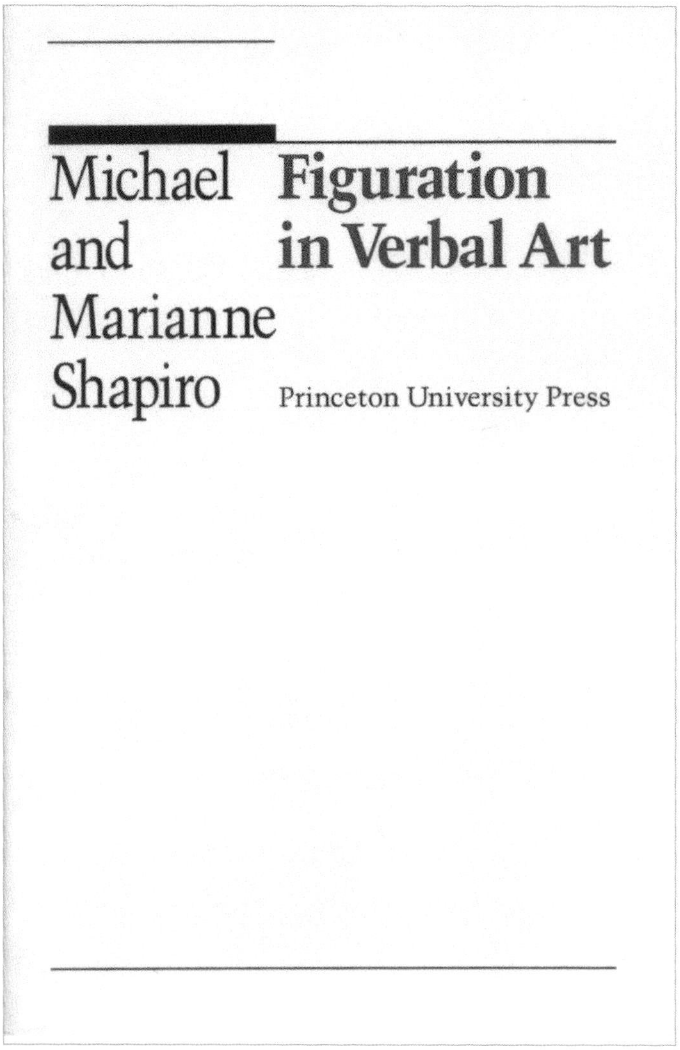

Michael
and
Marianne
Shapiro

Figuration
in Verbal Art

Princeton University Press

*Casebound in gray
bookcloth with gold foil
stamping on the spine;
Two-color offset
lithograph dustjacket;
6.25"x9.5"*

6.

FIGURATION IN VERBAL ART
[COAUTHOR, MICHAEL SHAPIRO].
PP. XV, 286. PRINCETON, N. J.:
PRINCETON UNIVERSITY PRESS, 1988.

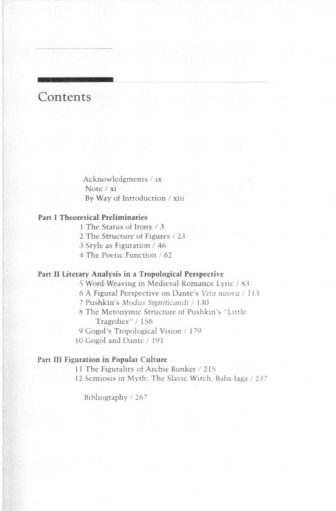

Contents

A highly atypical publication for the Princeton University Press list of the time, this book even includes a photograph of the authors on the back flap, taken in Berkeley in the fall of 1980, when both were visiting professors at the University of California.

Some encomia:

"In a brilliant synthesis the authors link Jakobson's structuralism with Peirce's theory of signs to produce a theory compatible with recent work on rhetoric, but able to surmount some of that work's inability to deal with historical and cultural questions. The book is an unusual combination of sophisticated theory with exemplary readings of particular works from American, Russian, and Italian popular and high culture."

— Michael Holquist, *Yale University*
(from the jacket flap)

"The Shapiros are among the few who have made good on Saussure's desire to make the scientific study of language a fundamentally semiotic one. Although this book can be placed under the general rubric of cognitive linguistics, it is much more interested in the semiotic nature of verbal creativity. It is a masterful analysis of 'figurative verbal art' (poetry, myth, etc.). To the best of my knowledge no such comprehensive work has previously existed."

— Marcel Danesi, in *The Semiotic
Review of Books* 1:1 (1990)

"The authors convincingly argue the close link between style and troping strategies, drawing upon a wide range of cultural and literary examples to clarify the *signum's* role as both a poetic trope and as a cultural *datum*. The final chapter of the first section offers not only an elaborative reprise of the earlier essays' discussions of asymmetrical signata and ranking, but also, to date, one of the most cohesive revisions of Jakobson's work on poetic function. This final theoretical essay, most heavily influenced by Peirce's view that the sign's being resides in 'the power to bring about a determination of a Matter' (79), is a *tour de force* of independent erudition in the meeting between linguistics and poetry."

— H. Wayne Storey, in *Romance Philology* 46:3 (1993)

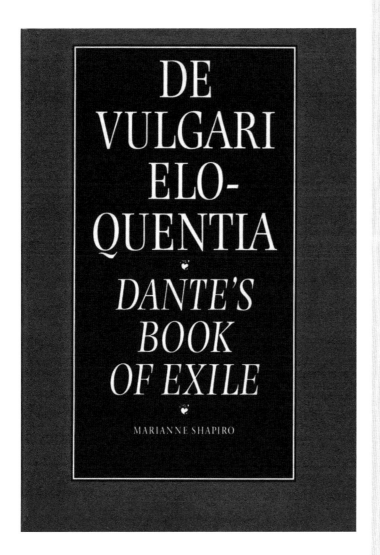

Casebound in violet bookcloth with black stamping on the spine; Two-color offset lithograph dustjacket; 6.0"x9.5"

7.

DE VULGARI ELOQUENTIA,
DANTE'S BOOK OF EXILE.
PP. XIV, 277. LINCOLN:
UNIVERSITY OF NEBRASKA PRESS, 1990.

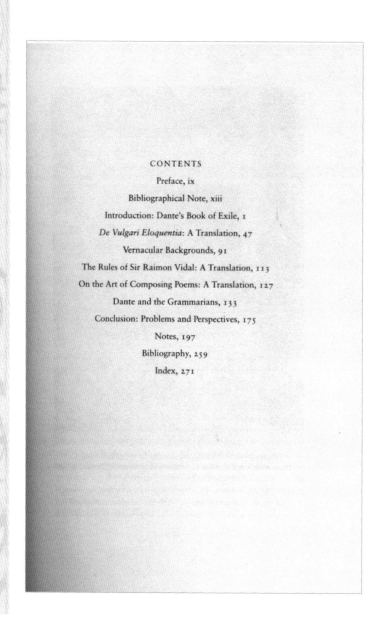

CONTENTS

While taking issue with the style of Marianne's translation, the most ringing words of praise of this work are sounded nevertheless by a fellow translator of *DVE*:

> "Broadly speaking, there have, up to now, been two main approaches to the fragmentary and more than somewhat problematic text that we call the *DVE*: the first sees it as simply another stage in the intellectual and literary development of Dante Alighieri, and relates it to the achieved poetic precedent of the *Vita nuova* and the *Rime*, on the one hand, while

seeing it as also being premonitory of the *Commedia*, on the other; the second, meanwhile, seeks to examine it in the light of other late medieval writings in the same domain of ideas, and to treat the fact of its Dantean authorship as largely incidental, if not actually as a dangerous distraction. No one writing in English, before Professor Shapiro, has attempted to unite the two approaches into a coherent and inclusive treatment, or come anything like as close as she does to triumphant success.

"What might be called the 'intrinsic' aspect of Shapiro's reading—that in which she interprets the *DVE* in the context of Dante's other works and their perceived thematic concerns—is grounded, as her title proclaims, in the concept of exile. In her first chapter (1–46), she conducts a searching inquiry into the political subtext of what often appears, on the surface of Dante's treatise, to be straightforward literary criticism or historical linguistics. By attending closely to the textual minutiae of the *DVE*—technical lexicon, illustrative examples, disposition of the argument—Shapiro is able to show, with wonderful lucidity, that this abbreviated *opusculum*, for all its superficial objectivity and detachment, is in fact charged to the full with the agonized intensity of Dante's personal experience of exile from Florence. Politics and poetry, all too easily placed at opposite poles of the intellectual compass (in the Middle Ages as today), are thus seen to be indissolubly linked, in Dante's conception, through their common reliance on the mechanics of language and the practice of ethics. There is no facile distinction to be made here: and Shapiro's penetrating analysis reveals, surely beyond possibility of refutation, that the connection is further strengthened by the centrality, in the *DVE* as in all Dante's work after 1301, of what is at once, for him, the metaphor and the literal reality of exile.

"The rest of the book proceeds to undertake an 'extrinsic' reading of the *DVE*, in which Dante's treatise is seen in the company of analogous and roughly contemporary writings by other authors and from other, albeit associated, linguistic and literary cultures. In a chapter entitled 'Vernacular Backgrounds' (91–112), Shapiro studies some of Dante's predecessors as analysts and explicators of vernacular language-theory and poetic technique: she focuses, in particular, on two Catalan handbooks of Provençal poetics, the *Razos de trobar* of Raimon Vidal (ca. 1200) and *De la doctrina de compondre dictatz* (late thirteenth century), attributable to Joifre de Foixà. Each of these is examined in some depth and then presented complete (113–31), in English translation. Shapiro's attention to these little-known but by no means negligible works is motivated, however, by more than their mere inherent interest or temporal proximity to the *DVE* (much greater in the case of the *Doctrina*, of course, than in that of the *Razos*): she holds, in fact, both that Dante knew these works (and others like them) directly, in one version or another, and that this direct influence 'stimulated him to surpass them' (xi). She puts forward several good reasons for adopting this belief, and is brave enough to look the countervailing evidence squarely in the eye; and, as a result, it is hard indeed to dissent from the chapter's conclusion that 'the filiation of *De vulgari eloquentia* with the modest Catalan treatises emerges from the outline of their respective projects and their intensely modernist idiom' (112). It is a conclusion, finely judged and elegantly expressed, exemplary of all that is good about Shapiro's book.

"The best, however, is yet to be. Shapiro's chapter on 'Dante and the Grammarians' (133–74) will be essential reading for all who care about the intellectual 'background' (a misnomer if ever there was one) of Dante's work, and especially to those benighted few (at least, one hopes they are few) who are debarred by unfamiliarity with Italian from appreciating the fundamental work, in this area, of Maria Corti and her circle. Shapiro has read extensively in late medieval grammatical theory—the realm of medieval linguistic thought that she finds, plausibly enough, to be most compellingly relevant to the *DVE*—and her hard-earned mastery of so many obscure and frequently rebarbative texts enables her to perform an analysis, at once exhaustive and authoritative, of various key terms in the technical vocabulary of Dante's treatise. Though the principal and recurrent *point de repère* is Boethius of Dacia, Shapiro manages to identify numerous affinities between Dante's thinking and the whole tradition of speculative grammar, demonstrating most effectively both that the *DVE* deviates from the norms of contemporary rhetoric and poetics, in often fascinating ways, and that its originality is owed in large part precisely to Dante's contact with the thought of the Danish Boethius and his colleagues. By the end of this exhilarating foray into material still too little known to most Dantists, Shapiro has convincingly established the truth of her prefatory claim that 'if we transport ourselves into some approximation of Dante's cultural matrices, we need see no contradiction between the poet and the grammarian, only that the latter is finally encapsulated within the former' (x). A summarizing conclusion ('Problems and Perspectives,' 175–95) brings this impressive book to a fitting close.

"This is a book of unusual importance and value—especially to those of its readers, sure to be the majority, for whom the translations (at least that of the *DVE*) will not be its principal attraction—and that no reader seriously interested in the *DVE*, whether in its own right or in its relationship with other texts, can afford to pass it by. Shapiro's work has permanently changed the scholarly landscape: from now on, serious discussion of the *De vulgari eloquentia* in English begins here."

— Steven N. Botterill, in *Envoi* 3:2 (1992)

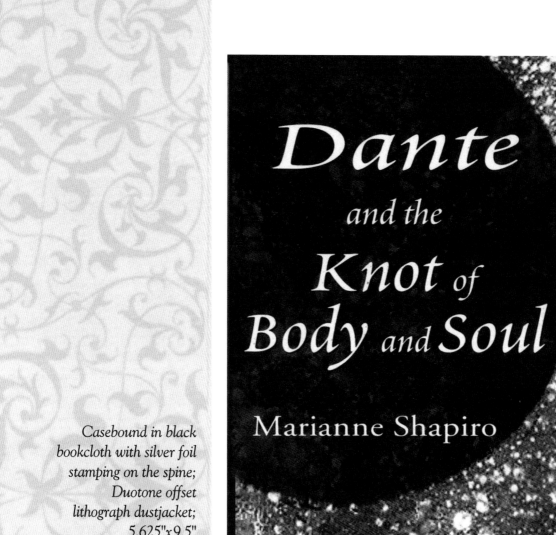

Casebound in black bookcloth with silver foil stamping on the spine; Duotone offset lithograph dustjacket; 5.625"x9.5"

8.

DANTE AND THE KNOT OF BODY AND SOUL.
PP. XIV, 220. NEW YORK:
ST. MARTIN'S PRESS, 1998.

Contents

Adjudged by one of the (anonymous) readers for St. Martin's Press as the product of "a first-rate Dante scholar working at the height of her powers," this book has yet to exert the influence it surely must in the long run, as reflected in the following assessments (the first two from the back cover):

> "Marianne Shapiro's new book makes a genuinely original contribution to Dante studies, sending us back to the *Commedia* with renewed appreciation and understanding. Throughout a complex, subtle, illuminating, and wide-ranging analysis, she never loses sight of the crucial fact that Dante's ideas about mankind and the universe derive their abiding fascination from his achievement as a poet."
>
> — Steven Botterill, *University of California, Berkeley*

"Thoroughly immersed in the *Comedy* and its cultural matrix, this strikingly original book abounds in surprising discoveries which compel us to rethink our fixed assumptions and see even the design of the poem itself with fresh eyes. Shapiro's work is sure to have a powerful effect on the way Dante is read and interpreted from now on."

— Paolo Cherchi, *University of Chicago*

"In this book the distinguished Italianist Marianne Shapiro, whose previous books include *Women Earthly and Divine in the Comedy of Dante, Hieroglyph of Time: The Petrarchan Sestina, The Poetics of Ariosto*, and *De vulgari eloquentia: Dante's Book of Exile*, addresses the issue of how, in the *Commedia*, disembodied souls are corporeally embodied or made flesh by Dante's art. According to Shapiro, Dante justifies the necessity of representing soul with body by the analogy between human language and the Incarnation. Unlike many contemporary *dantisti*, however, Shapiro does not dwell exclusively on the poet's use of theological and patristic sources, nor of classical ones (theoretical and literary), but, rather, on the textual interface between the theological and the literary. She argues, for instance, that Dante's sensorial representation of the soul derives from Virgil essentially but that the figures are rendered in different degrees of materiality, that the rules change or bend. This apparent incoherence results from the fact that the vision of the *Commedia* is necessarily composed of images; poetry provides what the philosophical arguments at Dante's disposal left incomplete.

"There is much to admire here, especially in the theoretical subtlety and sophistication of Shapiro's analyses."

— Olivia Holmes, in *Speculum* 76:4 (2001)

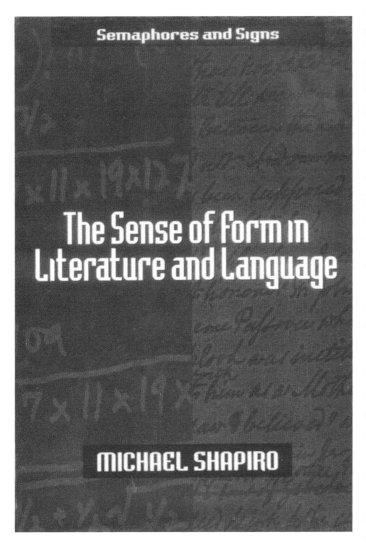

Semaphores and Signs

The Sense of Form in Literature and Language

MICHAEL SHAPIRO

Casebound in black bookcloth with gold foil stamping on the spine; Duotone offset lithograph dustjacket; 5.625"x9.5"

9.

*THE SENSE OF FORM
IN LITERATURE AND LANGUAGE*
[COAUTHOR, MICHAEL SHAPIRO].
SEMAPHORES AND SIGNS. PP. VIII, 215.
NEW YORK: ST. MARTIN'S PRESS, 1998.

CONTENTS

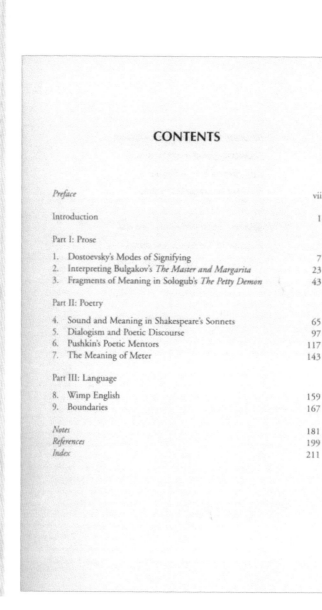

The genesis and publication history of this book is partly obscured by the fact that Marianne's name is missing from the cover and title page. This came about because she all too modestly insisted that her contributions to the essays did not merit equal recognition. Nothing could have been further from the truth (this omission has now been rectified in the second, expanded edition; see below). The encomia for the author of the first edition (the first two from the back cover) must, therefore, be read as applying to Marianne as well:

"Shapiro is in many ways a unique figure on the American scholarly scene, a powerful reader as much at home in technical literature as he is in the intricacies of formal poetics. I believe we are on the cusp of a move from externally oriented criticism to more internally organized reading; Shapiro's book might well come to be regarded as a canary in the mineshaft of literary scholarship. Anyone seriously interested in theoretical discussions of the relation between linguistics and literature will be drawn to the book."

— Michael Holquist, Professor of Comparative Literature,
Yale University

"Time and again, Shapiro achieves a synthesis of the particular and the universal, as careful analysis of detail, gathered from a dazzling, truly global array of sources, dovetails effortlessly into a judicious deduction of the principle that applies in each of the literary works he analyzes."

— Victor Terras, Professor Emeritus of Slavic Languages and
Comparative Literature, *Brown University*

"Michael Shapiro's book demonstrates the enormous scope of scholarly activities to which a Peircian approach can give rise. It is also a testament to the author's prodigious learning and expertise. To write essays on subjects ranging from 'Wimp English' to 'Dostoevsky's Modes of Signifying' is a feat in itself and one that will stretch the limits of most readers, this reviewer included."

— Andrew Barratt, in *Slavic Review* 59:4 (2000)

Higher Learning

a novel by

Marianne Shapiro

Perfect binding; process color offset lithograph dustjacket; 5.25"x8.0"

10.

HIGHER LEARNING, A NOVEL.

311 PP. CHARLESTON, S.C.: BOOK SURGE, 2004.

Marianne definitely had a flair for fiction, but this book could not find a publisher in her lifetime, so it was prepared by me for publication posthumously. Academic readers (see www.higherlearninganovel.com) praised it:

> "A delightful, scathing, and oh-so-true *roman à clef*. I have been telling everyone I know about this novel. It warmed my heart with its cheerfully unsentimental skewering of some that is best and all that is worst about academe. The author doesn't miss a trick: the academic in-fighting, the departmental hierarchy, the pretentious jargon of multiculturalists, the insidious 'arguments' of postmodernism, the unprincipled careerists, the spoiled and disaffected undergraduates, the harried and terrified grad students, the political overlapping with fundraising, the few, small islands of loyalty and sanity amid faddism, and the near-perfect inability of anyone to acknowledge aloud the truth of what was happening around them. It's all there."

> — Michael Gleason, *Millsaps College*

> "Marianne Shapiro's *Higher Learning* is a delight: it's smart, intriguing and at times uproariously funny. Nothing in higher education is safe from satire in this book. And in addition to all the clever and erudite humor, it's also a darned good mystery."

> — Norris Frederick,
> *Queens University of Charlotte*

> "Much more than a murder mystery laced with sex and intrigue, Marianne Shapiro's novel is a funny and yet withering satire on the foibles and hypocrisies of the contemporary American academy. A must-read for all college students, professors, and administrators—especially those who fancy themselves politically correct."

> — Michael Cabot Haley,
> *University of Alaska Anchorage*

> "Marianne Shapiro's *Higher Learning* is a highly original view of academic life, more brilliantly satirical than, say, the novels of David Lodge. Written by one of the world's greatest Dante scholars, it is a roman à clef and

a detective novel. Every line is barbed with wit — it's simply bloody funny!!"

— G. J. Barker-Benfield,
State University of New York at Albany

"The cover of Marianne Shapiro's novel *Higher Learning* shows a cracked ivory tower looking like an old telescope pointing to the foundations of the American university. Indeed, the modern pirates are underground like sewer rats and wear gowns, and their (twin) eye patches prevent them from seeing any kind of truth. The enigmatic motto of the book, *Cui prodest*, makes one think of the movie of some years back, *Kramer vs. Kramer*. The movie is a sharp vivisection of the American divorce, but in Europe it was taken as a totally imaginary world, and this was highly appreciated, because who could cook up such a fantastic world! The indications of the reactions to Marianne Shapiro's work seem to point to a similar split, viz. those who know academe and those who don't. Those who don't cannot believe that the ivory towers rest on dirty clay, although the book is extremely good reading. . . . Those who do know this 'sage' world refuse to see themselves parodied to a pulp, and ignore the *vivisectio sagax* in the book. Since Marianne Shapiro's book exposes the flim-flam operators and academic confidence men, of course they want to ignore it. The beauty of Marianne Shapiro's book is that it can be read without realizing the ironic total poverty of the modern American university. It provides mystery, intrigue, and satire, served with wit and charm. She does not overdo the scathing that would have been justified. But there it is for the initiated: secret societies of sham megalomaniacs and dim-witted failed scholars in positions of power, against whom the remaining 5% do not have a chance. And there, underground, students are molded and want to be molded into the insects of the 95%. The book is a novel, but at the same time a perspicacious sociological study. Great on both levels!"

— Raimo Anttila, *University of California, Los Angeles*

*Casebound;
two-color offset
lithograph self cover;
6.125"x9.25"*

II.

*From the Critic's Workbench:
Essays in Literature and Semiotics.*
Comp. & ed. Michael Shapiro. Pp. xii,
522. New York: Peter Lang, 2005.

Table of Contents

The essays in this volume were selected by me to demonstrate not only Marianne's broad sweep as a comparatist, medievalist, and Renaissance scholar but to put into print several unpublished manuscripts and notes from her Nachlass, including chapters 1, 2, 6, 7, 8, 11, 17, and 19. In all but one case, these were papers that Marianne had herself completed but did not seek to publish for one or another reason. Chapter 1 constitutes analyses of the *Aeneid* jotted down over several years to be used as raw material for a kind of self-help book on leadership for corporate executives, using Aeneas in particular as a model. Chapter 17 comprises notes prepared for me to use in a course I regularly taught at Brown on the Russian novel. These two chapters were put into publishable form as part of my editorial work on the volume.

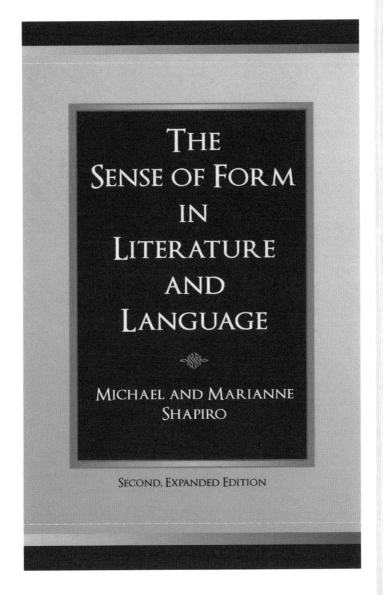

*Perfect binding;
process color offset
lithograph self cover;
5.5"x8.5"*

12.

*THE SENSE OF FORM
IN LITERATURE AND LANGUAGE*
[COAUTHOR, MICHAEL SHAPIRO].
2ND, EXPANDED ED. PP. XXI, 373.
SCOTTS VALLEY, CALIF.: CREATESPACE,
2009.

CONTENTS

This edition explicitly reinstates Marianne as the coauthor.

Here are (from the back cover, but in their full original versions) the book's endorsements:

"A work of art is constituted by compositional forms, which operate on many levels but remain implicit and unrecognized even as they affect us. These colorful essays by Michael and Marianne Shapiro bring such hidden forms to light. They increase our enjoyment of the art object and help us understand the combinatorial possibilities of human intelligence. The studies exhibit philosophical insight and wide-ranging knowledge of Russian literature, along with a sense of the complexities of ordinary speech and a structural understanding of Shakespeare's sonnets. They make the miracle of language more vividly present to us."

— Robert Sokolowski, Elizabeth Breckenridge Caldwell Professor of Philosophy, *Catholic University of America*

"It would be hard to identify a problem more central to the investigation of language and literature than that of the relationship between form and meaning (indeed, the cluster of problems pertaining to this relationship, not least of all, How does form as such secure a foothold for meaning, a basis from which the ascent to ever higher levels of significance can be negotiated? and, How does meaning in its myriad manifestations depend upon, and contribute to, our perception and alteration of form?). It is, in brief, hard to name a more central question for either the linguist or the student of literature, indeed, for anyone truly interested in language or literature. It is impossible, for me at least, to identify two inquirers who bring to this and related questions a more unique combination of literary sensitivity and linguistic erudition, a more relevant set of interpretive skills and theoretical expertise, than Marianne and Michael Shapiro do in this book. *The Sense of Form* is a work unto itself: it stands on its own feet, moving deftly from detailed analyses of specific literary works to an encompassing account of our most basic linguistic competencies – and back again. Read in light of Michael Shapiro's *The Sense of Grammar* (1983) and *The Sense of Change* (1991), however, it conveys an even deeper significance and richness. Among its diverse achievements, let me highlight but one other: Bakhtin's principle of dialogism has never been more insightfully explored or arrestingly exemplified than in *The Sense of Form*."

— Vincent Colapietro, Liberal Arts Research Professor, *Pennsylvania State University*

"*The Sense of Form in Literature and Language* is a masterful application of structuralist theory and Peirce's semeiotic to an impressive range of literary genres, authors, and periods. Michael and Marianne Shapiro argue convincingly for an iconic, diagrammatic relation between sound and meaning, against the Saussurean thesis of the arbitrariness of the sign. Whether it is their analysis of Shakespeare's sonnets, the Russian masters, Italian and Provençal literature, meter, or contemporary language patterns, they impress the reader with how the form and sound shape of language matters in understanding the meaning of the text. The second, expanded edition allows us to see more clearly the important contributions of Marianne Shapiro to this work."

— James J. Liszka, Dean, College of Arts and Sciences, Professor of Philosophy, *University of Alaska Anchorage*

II. Chapters in Books

1. "The Married Woman Scholar," *Careers and Couples: An Academic Question* (Publication of the MLA Commission on the Status of Women in the Profession), ed. L. Hoffman and G. de Sole, 25–29. New York: Modern Language Association, 1976.

2. "*Tenson* et *partimen*: la tenson fictive" ["*Tenso* and *partimen*: The Fictive Tenso"], *Proceedings of the Fourteenth International Congress of Romance Linguistics and Philology*, ed. A. Vàrvaro, V, 287–302. Amsterdam: Benjamins, 1981.

3. "Preliminaries to a Semiotics of Ballet," *The Sign in Music and Literature*, ed. W. Steiner, 216–227. Austin: The University of Texas Press, 1981.

4. "The Adynaton in Petrarch's Sestinas," *Dante, Petrarch, Boccaccio: Studies in the Italian Trecento in Honor of Charles S. Singleton*, ed. A. S. Bernardo and A. L. Pellegrini, 231–253. Binghamton, N. Y.: Medieval and Renaissance Texts and Studies, 1983.

5. "Matfre Ermengaud," *Dictionary of the Middle Ages*, ed. J. R. Strayer, IV, 506–507. New York: Charles Scribner's Sons, 1984.

6. "Sestina," *The Spenser Encyclopedia*, ed. A. C. Hamilton, 637–638. Toronto: University of Toronto Press, 1990.

7. "[Inferno] XXV," *Special Issue: Lectura Dantis Virginiana*, Vol. 1, Dante's *Divine Comedy*: Introductory Readings I: *Inferno*, ed. T. Wlassics, 319–331[= Supplement, *Lectura Dantis*, 6]. Charlottesville: University of Virginia, 1990.

8. "Figuration," *The New Princeton Encyclopedia of Poetry and Poetics*, ed. A. Preminger and T. V. F. Brogan, 408–409. Princeton, N. J.: Princeton University Press, 1993.

9. "Repetition," *The New Princeton Encyclopedia of Poetry and Poetics*, ed. A. Preminger and T. V. F. Brogan, 1035–1037. Princeton, N. J.: Princeton University Press, 1993.

10. "[Purgatorio] XI," *Special Issue: Lectura Dantis Virginiana*, Vol. 2, Dante's *Divine Comedy*: Introductory Readings II: *Purgatory* (= *Lectura Dantis*, Supplement, 12), ed. T. Wlassics, 158–168. Charlottesville: University of Virginia, 1993.

11. "Pushkin and Petrarch" [coauthor, Michael Shapiro], *American Contributions to the Eleventh International Congress of Slavists*, ed. R. Maguire and A. Timberlake, 154–169. Columbus, Ohio: Slavica, 1993.

12. "Traces of Pushkin and Other Russian Classics in *The Petty Demon* [coauthor, Michael Shapiro], *Alexander Lipson In Memoriam*," ed. C. Gribble et al., 250–275. Columbus, Ohio: Slavica, 1994.

13. "[Paradiso] XVII," *Special Issue: Lectura Dantis Virginiana*, Vol. 3, Dante's *Divine Comedy*: Introductory Readings III: *Paradiso* [= *Lectura Dantis*, 16-17], ed. T. Wlassics, 246–265. Charlottesville: University of Virginia, 1995.

14. "Arnaut Daniel," "Oderisi da Gubbio," "Omberto Aldobrandeschi," "Provenzan Salvani," "Sordello," [five entries in] *The Dante Encyclopedia*, ed. R. Lansing, 65–66, 658, 660, 718, 794–795. New York: Garland Press, 2000.

15. "On the Rôle of Rhetoric in the Convivio," *Dante: The Critical Complex*, ed. R. Lansing, Vol. 3, *Dante and Philosophy: Nature, the Cosmos, and the Ethical Imperative*, 56–82. New York: Routledge, 2002. [rpt. of III.32 below]

III. Articles in Journals

1. "The *Storie ferraresi* of Giorgio Bassani," *Italica*, 49 (1972), 30–48.

2. "Poetry and Politics in the *Comento* of Lorenzo il Magnifico," *Renaissance Quarterly*, 26 (1973), 444–453.

3. "Petrarch, Lorenzo il Magnifico, and the Latin Elegiac Poets," *Romance Notes*, 15 (1973), 172–175.

4. "Society and the Theme of Praise in the *Vita Nuova*," *Neophilologus*, 57 (1973), 330–340.

5. "An Old French Source for Ugolino?" *Dante Studies*, 92 (1974), 129–148.

6. "Semiramis in *Inf. V*," *Romance Notes*, 16 (1974), 455–456.

7. "The Fictionalization of Bertran de Born (*Inf. XXVIII*)," *Dante Studies*, 9 (1974), 107–116.

8. "Spatial Relationships in Dante's *Vita Nuova*," *Romance Notes*, 16 (1974), 708–711.

9. "Mirror and Portrait: The Structure of *Il libro del Cortegiano*," *Journal of Medieval and Renaissance Studies*, 5 (1975), 37–61.

10. "*The Gran Lombardo*: Vittorini and Dante," *Italica*, 62 (1975), 70–77.

11. "The Petrarchan *selva* Revisited: Sestina XXII," *Neuphilologische Mitteilungen*, 77 (1976), 144–160.

12. "The Figure of the Watchman in the Provençal Erotic *alba*," *MLN*, 91 (1976), 607–639.

13. "Addendum: Christological Language in *Inferno XXXIII*," *Dante Studies*, 94 (1976), 141–143.

14. "Brunetto's Race (*Inf. XV*)," *Dante Studies*, 95 (1977), 153–156.

15. "Robert Saverio Pastena, 1949-1975," *Yale Italian Studies*, 1 (1977), 144–145.

16. "The Provençal *Trobairitz* and the Limits of Courtly Love," *Signs*, 3 (1978), 560–571.

17. "*Fols Naturaus*: The Born Fool as Literary Type," *Romance Notes*, 19 (1978), 243–247.

18. "A Dantesque *alba* by Cerveri de Girona," *Kentucky Romance Quarterly*, 25 (1978), 509–514.

19. "Bassani's Ironic Mode," *The Canadian Journal of Italian Studies*, 1 (1978), 146–152.

20. "Figurality in the *Vita Nuova*: Dante's New Rhetoric," *Dante Studies*, 97 (1979), 107–127.

21. "John Ashbery: *The New Spirit*," *Water Table*, 1 (1980), 58–73.

22. "The Semiotics of Archie Bunker," *Ars Semeiotica*, 3 (1980), 159–180.

23. "Dante and the Painting of Nature," *Dante Studies*, 99 (1981), 133–144.

24. "The Decline of *joi* in the Provençal *planh*," *Kentucky Romance Quarterly*, 28 (1981), 351–369.

25. "*Purgatorio XXX*: Arnaut at the Summit," *Dante Studies*, 100 (1982), 71–76.

26. "Revelation and the Vials of Sanity in the *Orlando Furioso*," *Romance Notes*, 22 (1982), 329–334.

27. "From Atlas to Atlante," *Comparative Literature*, 35 (1983), 323–350.

28. "Perseus and Bellerophon in *Orlando Furioso*," *Modern Philology*, 81 (1983), 109–130.

29. "*Entrebescar los motz*: Word-Weaving in Medieval Romance Lyric," *Zeitschrift für romanische Philologie*, 100 (1984), 355–383.

30. "How Narrators Report Speech," *Language and Style*, 17 (1984), 67–78.

31. "The Status of Irony," *Stanford Literature Review*, 2 (1985), 5–26.

32. "On the Rôle of Rhetoric in the *Convivio*," *Romance Philology*, 40 (1986), 38–64.

33. "Gogol and Dante," *Modern Language Studies*, 17 (1987), 37–54.

34. "Ecphrasis in Virgil and Dante," *Comparative Literature*, 42 (1990), 97–115.

35. "Dante and the Grammarians," *Zeitschrift für romanische Philologie*, 105 (1989), 498–528.

36. "*Ami et Amile* and Myths of Divine Twinship," *Romanische Forschungen*, 102 (1990), 131–148.

37. "Virgilian Representation in Dante," *Lectura Dantis*, 5 (1989), 19–40.

38. "Dialogism and the Addressee in Lyric Poetry" [coauthor, Michael Shapiro], *University of Toronto Quarterly*, 61 (1992), 392–413.

39. "*Homo Artifex*: A Rereading of *Purgatorio XI*," *Lectura Dantis*, 10 (1992), 59–69.

40. "Wimp English" [coauthor, Michael Shapiro], *American Speech*, 68 (1993), 327–330.

41. "The Trinity as Semiotic," *The Peirce Seminar Papers*, 2 (1994), 209–229.

42. "Dante's Twofold Representation of the Soul," *Lectura Dantis*, 18–19 (1996), 49–90.

43. "'Men che di rose e più che di viole' (Purg. 32.78): The Widowed Crown," *Lectura Dantis*, 20–21 (1997), 59–77.

44. "Rereading Dostoevskij's *Dvojnik*," Russian Literature, 56 (2004), 441–482.

45. "Literary-Historical Consequences of the Russian Non-Renaissance in a Comparative Context" [coauthor, Michael Shapiro], *Russian Literature*, 66 (2009), 443-455.

IV. MISCELLANEA

A. Book reviews

1. "*Dante Studies 1966-1968.*" *Romance Philology*, 24 (1971), 538–539.

2. "Thomas Bergin, *Perspectives on Dante.*" *Romance Philology*, 25 (1971), 259–260.

3. "Marco Pecoraro, *Saggi vari da Dante al Tommaseo.*" *Romance Philology*, 26 (1973), 622–626.

4. "*Dante Studies 1969.*" *Romance Philology*, 28 (1974), 265–266.

5. "Jean Pépin, *Dante et la tradition de l'allégorie.*" *Romance Philology*, 28 (1974), 233–236.

6. "Arshi Pipa, *Dante and Montale.*" *Romance Philology*, 28 (1975), 420–422.

7. "*Studi di filologia romanza offerti a Silvio Pellegrini.*" *Romance Philology*, 29 (1975), 265–273.

8. "Charles S. Singleton (ed. & tr.), *Dante Alighieri, The Divine Comedy: Purgatorio.*" *Romanic Review* 67 (1976), 81–83.

9. "G. D'Aronco, *Letteratura popolare italiana.*" *Romance Philology*, 30 (1976), 427–428.

10. "Alberto Del Monte (ed.), *Conti di antichi cavalieri.*" *Romance Philology*, 30 (1977), 557–558.

11. "Vincenzo Cioffari (ed.), *Guido da Pisa's Expositiones et glose super Comediam Dantis.*" *Romanic Review*, 69 (1978), 257–258.

12. "Thomas A. Sebeok (ed.), *Sight, Sound, and Sense.*" *Language*, 55 (1979), 495–496.

13. "George Steiner, *On Difficulty.*" *Language*, 55 (1979), 754–755.

14. "Michael Riffaterre, *Semiotics of Poetry*." *Language*, 56 (1980), 456–458.

15. "E. L. Epstein, *Language and Style*." *Language*, 56 (1980), 477–478.

16. "Judith Hanna, *To Dance Is Human*." *Ars Semeiotica*, 4 (1981), 97–106.

17. "Giuseppe Mazzotta, *Dante, Poet of the Desert*." *Italica*, 59 (1982), 57–58.

18. "Sergio Corsi, II '*modus digressivus*' *Nella Commedia*." *Italica*, 67 (1990), 231–234.

19. "John Saly, *Dante's Paradiso*." *Lectura Dantis*, 6 (1990), 150–153.

20. "Dino S. Cervigni (ed.), *Dante and Modern American Criticism*." *Lectura Dantis*, 9 (1991), 139–141.

21. "Davy A. Carozza and H. James Shey, *Petrarch's Secretum with Introduction, Notes, and Critical Anthology*." *Italica*, 69 (1992), 76–79.

22. "Jean Fisette, *Introduction à la sémiotique de C. S. Peirce* [= "The Rudiments of Peirce's Semiotic"]." *Semiotica*, 104 (1995), 241–244.

B. Translations

1. "The Words of Leonardo, " in *The Unknown Leonardo*, ed. Ladislao Reti, 293–300. New York: McGraw-Hill, 1974.

APPENDICES

APPENDIX A

Curriculum Vitae of Marianne Shapiro

1940	Born Marianne Irene Goldner, April 14, Budapest (Hungary)
1942	Immigrated with parents to New York
1946–54	P. S. 146, Washington Heights, New York
1954–57	High School of Music and Art, West 135th St., New York; Diploma, 1957
1957–60	Barnard College, New York; B. A. in French and in Italian [double major], 1960
1960–61	Manhattan
1961–62	Radcliffe College, Harvard University; A. M. in French, 1962
1962–68	Graduate Student, Department of Italian, Columbia University
1963	Instructor, Brooklyn Navy Yard, Summer Term
	Instructor in Summer Sessions, Columbia University
1964	Instructor, Manhattan School of Music, Spring Semester
1964–65	Fulbright Scholar, Universities of Rome and Florence (Italy)
1965	Instructor in Summer Sessions, Columbia University
1967	Married Michael Shapiro, June 25; moved to Los Angeles, Calif.
1968	Birth of daughter Abigail, October 14
	Ph.D. in Italian, Columbia
1968–70	Assistant Professor of Italian, UCLA

1971–72	Professor of Italian, Sarah Lawrence College
1972–75	Assistant Professor of Italian, Yale University
1975–78	Associate Professor of Italian, Yale University
1978–80	Los Angeles
1980	Manhattan
1980–83	Associate Professor of Italian, New York University
1983–86	Manhattan
1986	Visiting Associate Professor of Comparative Literature, University of California, Berkeley (fall term)
1986–90	Manhattan
1990–92	Visiting Professor of Comparative Literature, Brown University
1992–93	Manhattan and Manchester Center, Vermont
1993–94	Visiting Lecturer in Romance Languages and Literatures, Boston College
1994	Visiting Professor of Italian Studies, Brown University (fall term)
1995–97	Adjunct Professor of Italian Studies, Brown University
1998–2000	Visiting Scholar in Italian Studies, Brown University
2000–03	Manhattan and Manchester Center, Vermont
2003	Died at home, June 3, Manchester Center, Vermont

Excerpt from
*Palimpsest of Consciousness:
Authorial Annotations of My Wife
the Metaphysician, or Lady Murasaki's Revenge*
by Michael Shapiro
(Charleston, S. C.: BookSurge Publishing, 2006), pp. 13–24

My wife, the metaphysician. There was a life before she married me, of course. She was born Marianne (Hebrew name, Miriam) Irene Goldner, on April 14, 1940, into a Jewish family in Budapest (Hungary). (She did not use either Miriam or Irene as an adult.) Her parents were Dezsö and Edith Goldner (née [von] Freudiger). Edith Freudiger was also born in Budapest. Her mother tongue was Hungarian, but she also had fluent German from her parents and from the "Fräulein" (that's the way my mother-in-law always referred to her) whom they employed for their children as a tutor. Her father had gotten a baronry by virtue of his wealth and social stature (he was a factory owner), hence the "von" which Edith also used on occasion. (My father typically referred to her somewhat facetiously in Russian as *baronessa*.) Dezsö [= Desiderius] Goldner was a lumber merchant of humble forebears (Marianne always joked that her father was descended from Jewish horse thieves) from Kosice (alias Košice), a city in eastern Slovakia, which was part of Hungary from the eleventh century until 1918. In addition to Hungarian, Slovak, and German, the three primary languages in the Kosice of his day, my father-in-law spoke Yiddish and even Rusyn, a Trans-Carpathian dialect of Ukrainian in common use in this multi-ethnic mileu. The union of Edith and Dezsö was an arranged marriage, a perfectly quotidian matter among Orthodox Jews of a certain socioeconomic class. But the disparity in backgrounds between Budapest and Kosice (among other things) was to have its emotional reverberations in the vicissitudes of family life of these refugees, whose daughter chafed under the strictures of Orthodoxy and yearned for a time when she could throw them off once and for all.

Marianne immigrated to America in 1942. She and her mother went from Hungary to Portugal, where they boarded a ship that transported them to New York via Brazil. Her father, who was in London on business when the war broke out and was stranded there alone, joined them in America directly from England. They settled in Upper Manhattan, in Castle Village, a group of high-rise apartments on Cabrini Boulevard populated largely by German Jews (now almost totally Dominican). The family was enlarged in 1943 by the birth of Marianne's younger brother, George (now a curator at the Metropolitan Museum of Art), which occasioned another important addition in the person of Amalia Jaffa—known forever as "Molly"—a German-Jewish bookkeeper from Lübeck, who had fled Nazi Germany and come to New York via England. Molly, a lifelong spinster with a good sense of humor and a German accent the kids made fun of, became the children's nanny and general *major domo*, staying with the family as a devoted retainer until her death in the '80s. (This is one of the remarkable parallelisms in Marianne's and my biographies that will prefigure the arc of our destinies.) Deszö tried a variety of businesses with limited success before settling down to buying and selling real estate (at which he was more than successful). The family eventually moved from Castle Village to West 72nd Street, then to Park Avenue.

Marianne was a precocious child, learning to read by the time she was four (with her father's help), simply because she couldn't stand the frustration of not knowing what it said on labels and other printed matter. She also showed an early aptitude for music, the piano in particular, and was playing Mozart Concertos on the radio by the time she was nine. Public school years before high school were accordingly a bore because she was always far more advanced than her fellow-students. The teachers didn't like her because she sat twiddling her thumbs, finishing assignments ahead of everybody else and waiting for the others to catch up (there was no "tracking" in those days). Also—which was far worse—she asked questions that the old-maid Irish teachers couldn't answer. Her mother—out of frustration more than anything—finally took her to Teachers College at Columbia to be tested. The results were perfectly predictable: she had a very high IQ, so high in fact that the psychologists were at a loss in counseling her mother. Nevertheless, her parents resisted sending her to a private school, even though Marianne kept agitating for it (and resented their intransigence far into adulthood); her father, in particular, didn't want to stick out among the group of his relatives that had survived the Holocaust and settled in New York, all of whose children went to public schools. But relief was on the way. Having been coached in math and science by her father, who at bottom was always proud of her intellectual distinction and wanted her to be a scientist rather than a homemaker in the Orthodox Jewish mode of her mother, Marianne passed the tough entrance exam and was accepted by the Bronx High School of Science, one of the three original specialized science high schools in New York. But her love of (and talent for) music impelled her in the direction of the High School of Music and Art (which was then located on 135th Street in Harlem), for which she also passed the competitive entrance exam. (Getting into Bronx Science *and* Music and Art was then— as it is now—an unheard of feat.) There, finally, as a pianist she throve among the other talented kids, including singers and painters and instrumentalists (she even learned to conduct the orchestra). Marianne had absolute pitch all her life and could play anything she heard on the piano. She graduated in 1957 and was awarded a New York State Regents Scholarship (the coveted merit scholarship in those days) for college study.

Marianne wanted to go to a conservatory and become a concert pianist but was thwarted in this ambition by her parents, who objected and made it clear that they would not support her in such a precarious career. So she took the line of least resistance and applied to several Eastern women's colleges.

Radcliffe was her first choice, but when the interviewer asked her, out of the blue, whether she had read *Marjorie Morningstar*, she knew that things weren't going to turn out well. (*O tempora, o mores*: thirty years later, our daughter, Abigail, another New York Jewish girl, was admitted early to Harvard-Radcliffe.) Marianne was accepted by Wellesley but settled for Barnard because of wanting to stay in New York. The years she was there (1957–60) coincided with the presidency of the formidable Millicent Carey McIntosh, an era when the girls still knitted in class and were "pinned" or sported engagement rings by the time they were juniors. Attendance at student assembly was mandatory. Marianne, who always hated organizations and corporate togetherness, shunned such rituals and mostly got away with it because she was clearly the brainiest and most talented student around. The courses and the instructors at Barnard were far from stimulating. (The only teachers—both in French—she ever mentioned with respect were Jeanne Varney Pleasants [French phonetics] and particularly Elizabeth Czoniczer [modern French literature].) She took a course in medieval art at Columbia with Meyer Schapiro, who stood out as a lecturer as well as an art historian. (In those days, female students were allowed to take courses at Columbia only if they weren't offered at Barnard.) Other than one summer at the Tanglewood Music Festival as a member of the chorus under Lorna Cooke de Varon, whom she always remembered with admiration as a super-competent chorusmistress (and whose daughter, Joanna, was my graduate student in the Slavic Department at UCLA in the '70s), Marianne spent her summers taking extra courses and graduated one year early in 1960, with a double major in French and in Italian, winning the Italian Prize that year for being the outstanding graduate.

A year of *dolce far niente* followed, during which she took odd jobs in New York before deciding to embark on a graduate program in French at Harvard and being awarded a Radcliffe Fellowship in 1961–62. (This coincided with my first year at Harvard as a graduate student in Slavic Languages and Literatures. Marianne always lamented the fact that we never met during that year, even though we had certain acquaintances in common who never thought to introduce us. She reckoned that if she had met me then, I would have kept her from leaving Harvard and making the fateful decision to switch to Italian for a Ph.D. instead of continuing with French—a field infinitely more hospitable to outsiders than the flagitiously insular Italian. Having taken it up at Music and Art in conjunction with her study of vocal music, Marianne already spoke Italian like a native—a native radio announcer, that is, because unlike actual Italians her speech bore no traces of a regional provenience.)

Marianne only spent one year in Cambridge, at the Graduate Center, a women's residence at 6 Ash Street. She sailed through the M. A. program because her French was that good. (She had learned it as a child in school and had gotten extra tutoring on her own. By the time she landed at Radcliffe, she spoke like a Parisian and could write pastiches of any French author at the snap of a finger). But she missed New York, and seeing that French was oversubscribed while Italian had a dearth of smart graduate students, she decided to go back to Columbia to pursue a Ph. D. in her other undergraduate degree field. (This was a decision she was to rue the rest of her life.)

The year 1962-63 was spent taking Italian graduate courses and then the Ph. D. qualifying exams. In the summer of 1963 she had the interesting experience of teaching Italian to a class of officers at the Brooklyn Navy Yard. Marianne remembers how eager they were to learn, and how they rose en masse from their seats to greet their instructor whenever she walked into class. Imagine the impact of that flourish on a (painfully shy) young woman of twenty-three!

In the spring of 1964, having started work on her doctoral dissertation (later published as her first book, *Woman Earthly and Divine in the Comedy of Dante* [1975]), Marianne taught Italian to undergraduates at the Manhattan School of Music and then went off to study in Italy for a year on a Fulbright Scholarship, first at the University of Rome (fall semester), then the University of Florence (spring). There wan't that much formal studying to be done: these were, after all, Italian universities, where *laissez faire* was the norm. So she soaked up the atmosphere and spoke Italian with a wide circle of friends. She did, however, also read omnivorously (as usual) and made a point of attending the lectures in Florence of the coryphaeus of Italian literary scholars, Gianfranco Contini, one of the few Italianists whose scholarship she esteemed throughout her working life.

The summer of 1965 found Marianne back in New York, so she taught Italian in the summer session at Columbia and continued to do research for her dissertation on the women characters in the *Comedy*. But the work wasn't going as well as it ought to have done. The academic year 1965–66 came and went without any real progress. Out of exasperation she turned to the psychologist Ethel Kardiner (wife of the eminent psychiatrist, Abram Kardiner) for professional advice. Conversations with a highly intelligent professional woman (they continued until ca. 1968) were a pleasure apart from any therapeutic benefits, but they did not help Marianne surmount the barriers (chiefly, lack of motivation) preventing her from writing a dissertation.

This is where I came in—to be specific, on December 30, 1966.

But before continuing, perhaps I should say something about Marianne's personality and appearance; also about the effect these features had on members of the opposite sex. She was shy with strangers but always a sparkling conversationalist when unleashed, full of effortless one-liners and original *bons mots*, to the point that one friend who knew her all our married life (Ben Benfield) urged me repeatedly and in all seriousness to record and transcribe what came from Marianne's mouth because, he insisted, it could be made into a publication as entertaining as anything in extant humor books. These linguistic productions came effortlessly, in a totally cliché-less (Marianne hated clichés), racy, inventive, lapidary idiom, unmistakably of her own construction, with perfect, unaccented diction and in a strong, somewhat deep yet mellifluous voice. (Her students often remarked that her lectures could be heard with no loss of comprehension by someone standing far down the hall with the classroom door closed.) What a delight to hear such speech—and from a beautiful woman!

As photographs will attest, Marianne was always beautiful, as a child and as an adult. But it was not a conventional beauty, even for a Jewish girl of her generation; rather, it was a special amalgam of the Magyar, the Slavic, and the Hebraic that is not often glimpsed nowadays (and which our daughter inherited). I have already described her hair, which framed the oval of a face whose olive skin color tended toward alabaster. She had a prominent nose (from her mother)—which she considered a defect but I found very attractive. Her eyes were dark brown in slightly narrowed sockets, and her lips, when pursed, described a small bow-knot. Her teeth were small. She had a good figure, was about 5' 4" in height, and weighed less than 120 lbs. on our wedding day. (Footnote: all of this without having spent one day in the gym her whole life; perspiration was considered unladylike by her mother, with her decidedly old-fashioned, Eastern European notions of propriety, hence no physical exertion except swimming being sanctioned. Marianne often quipped to me that, with my lifelong history of participation in athletics, I should have married someone more *sportive*.)

As she passed from adolescence into womanhood, men started taking notice and buzzed around her, although she paid them scant attention because of her inborn shyness. Her mother's plan was for her to marry an Orthodox man before she was out of her 'teens and to have a passel of children. She often rebuked Marianne for wearing her hair with a part down the middle because, said her Hungarian mater and self-appointed *arbiter elegantiarum*, it "made Marianne look like a schoolteacher," which meant that she would never "get a man" (the late '50s were still the days of old-maid schoolteachers). All the same, suitable young men were repeatedly maneuvered into place. (There were jokes told about how one aspirant for her hand showed up at the Goldners' door, expecting to take Marianne out on a date, only to be informed that she had already left for the evening with someone else!) Finally, to get her mother out of her hair, Marianne actually got engaged to one such suitor and even wore his engagement ring for a while. Naturally, she had no intention whatever of actually marrying the poor sap. In fact, she let the ring slip off her finger (by accident, she averred) and disappear down—a toilet! Luckily, it was retrieved by a resourceful plumber and was given back to its donor on some artful pretext for calling the whole thing off.

When I speak of the parallelism of our biographies determining the arc of our destinies, I mean this literally, not metaphorically. (Much later, after we were married and Marianne became conversant with the terminology of my philosophical hero, Charles Sanders Peirce, and could appreciate the reference, I often said to her that we were each other's "destined interpretant.") Thus, our first meeting on that day in December 1966 was no happenstance. It had been "prepared" in more ways than one.

Just after Christmas '66 I was in Manhattan for a week, having come from Los Angeles to give a paper at a conference, and was staying at my brother Isaac's apartment on West 101st Street. It was in a rental building co-owned at the time by Marianne's father. One of the other tenants was Marianne's cousin, Beate Gordon (née Sirota), who was known to my brother and me from our days in Japan. (Beate had grown up there; her father, Leo, was a Russian-Jewish refugee pianist and part of my parents' orbit; her mother, Gisela, was related to Marianne's mother's family through a link with the family of the conductor, Jascha Horenstein, who was born in Kiev. To complete the parallelism, it later transpired that Marianne and I were distantly related via her mother and my father, the link being the Horensteins and the Brodski family of Kiev [the sugar magnates = Russian *sakharozavodchiki*].) My brother and his wife were having a dinner party on December 30th, to which Beate and her husband had been invited. Knowing of my presence and thinking Marianne should meet me, Beate asked whether she could bring Marianne. Having nothing better to do, Marianne agreed when offered the chance.

Marianne often remarked later that she first caught sight of me at that party when I "suddenly materialized from behind a pillar." (Why this mattered one can only surmise [I never asked]; perhaps it was the suddenness—as in the French *coup de foudre* [?].) She was wearing a dress the color of wisteria (!), which I never forgot. We spent the whole evening talking to each other and to no one else. The next day was New Year's Eve, and Marianne already had a date, so we agreed that I would come over to her apartment on East 84th Street on New Year's Day. We spent nine hours together talking. I had to return to Los Angeles the following morning, but we wrote to each other. The one phrase that Marianne remembered more than once from the first letter I wrote her was: "It's as if you'd wiped out all other thoughts from my brain." Which was true, of course. She had. It reminded me of what my mother had told me of her first meeting with my father. Phone calls and more letters followed. I decided to come back to New York in February (1967) to see Marianne, with the intention of asking her to marry me. I stayed at the St. Moritz Hotel on Central Park South (now called the Ritz Carlton). When I revisited Marianne's apartment on East 84th, rang the buzzer, and was asked who it was, I answered "Dante Alighieri." I proposed. She accepted. (Later, Marianne always joked that she had to prompt me by saying: "So, when are we getting married?"). I was invited to dinner at her parents' apartment on Park Avenue. Rather than asking for his daughter's hand, I simply announced to her father that we had decided to get married. Her parents were thunderstruck. Marianne's mother confessed to me (much later, of course) that all the peripeteia with rejected suitors had made her utterly despair of seeing her daughter married.

We only saw each other nine times before we were married. Some of these occasions were in Los Angeles, when Marianne and her parents came to meet mine in the spring of 1967, and I took Marianne to a jeweler to choose an engagement ring. Naturally, the parents hit it off. Think of it: the foreign-born children of two sets of Jewish refugee parents—all four fluent speakers of German in addition to English, from a similar Old World milieu, the *fin de siecle* milieu of Budapest and Berlin and Moscow and St. Petersburg and Kiev—had been brought together in New York as an afterthought by a distant relative who had also been in Japan during the war. They had fallen in love at first sight and were now engaged to be married.

We were married on June 25, 1967, at the Hotel Pierre in New York (in the same ballroom as our daughter was to be married twenty-eight years later). Our honeymoon trip took us first to Martha's Vineyard and Nantucket Island; then to

Europe, the USSR, and finally Japan before flying to Los Angeles and the beginning of our life together. In Moscow my brother Joseph (more about him later) met us and accompanied us down to Sochi in Georgia, then back to Moscow, from which we flew in a giant Tupolev plane to Tokyo and stayed at the old Imperial Hotel (the one designed by Frank Lloyd Wright), just a year before it was torn down and replaced with its current nondescript namesake. It was a delight to be staying with Marianne in the Meiji-era hotel in whose arcades and lobbies I had gamboled many times as a child during the Occupation. (The Ernie Pyle Theatre across the street, which showed American movies for military personnel, was a favorite destination in those early postwar days.) I remember a sushi meal we had there—one of the first she ever had—at which Marianne devoured so many that she got sick and was put off sushi for months afterward. (It reminded me of the time as a child after the war and the food shortages when I consumed a whole can of mushrooms and couldn't eat them for a year.)

Speaking of culinary matters, my Taiwanese friends from the Kokusai Gakuyûkai organized a splendid Chinese lunch in honor of the newlyweds at the old Chinzanso Restaurant overlooking the beautiful Chinzan-so Gardens. It was a meal we never forgot for its Lucullan magnificence. A tour of Japan by train and bus followed, which included all the de rigueur sights. My postdoctoral year in 1965-66 had not included much traveling, so this trip with Marianne was the first good look since childhood at the country of my birth."

Appendix C

Book Proposal: *Constructing Leonardo*
by Marianne Shapiro

Constructing Leonardo will study and analyze the cultural image of Leonardo da Vinci, man and work, as it has been fashioned and elaborated from his lifetime to the present day. It begins by asking why Leonardo has been considered so often as somehow failed or flawed.

The book will show the power of written, spoken, painted, and advertised fictions to influence the shape of external reality. I will explore the possibility that Leonardo's androgynous personality accounts for the tendency to think of him as a magnificent failure, an idea that competes with his fame as a genius and creator of masterpieces. Androgyny as a concept shows how the truest, most essential part of an individual's cultural myth is his potential self, which might or might not be revealed by events in his life.

What are the "feminine" elements of personality that have coalesced into a popular composite image of Leonardo? These will be explored through a radical interrogation of the Leonardo tradition, as in films like "Mona Lisa" (1987) and popular songs, which serve to transfer to Leonardo elements generations of viewers have seen in the most "canonical" of the paintings.

The compass of the book emphasizes European and North American contributions to the image but will also include versions of Leonardo—and especially of his best known works of art—which derive from third world cultures, where they play an assisting role in the shaping of a modern civilization.

I intend largely to avoid rehearsals of art history (and theory) as they were practiced in Leonardo's time and to make the fullest use of "image-building" documents—for example, fictions, jingles, and doggerel as well as replicas of (and riffs on) paintings.

The book will examine the life of a human artistic icon to show the reciprocal relation between material we think we know on "authority" and our interpretation of that material. The life of Leonardo offers a major opportunity because it has neither a lack of documentation nor anything like a satisfying degree of it. Thus, while there is enough in his contemporary record for a beginning, its development presents a major retrospective of cultural movements on a world scale. The early biography by Vasari and accounts of Leonardo by Italian near-contemporaries yield to exponential growth in the course of the 19th and 20th centuries, the leading "learned" purveyor being Dmitri Merezhkovsky's *Romance of Leonardo da Vinci*, a fiction whose seminal influence determined Freud's own view and nearly forced his conclusions. Contemporaneous with these works is a host of popular travel guides and memoirs, even operettas, which functioned as transmitters of the "life." The career of Walter Pater is important in determining a whole school of reception, as well as other Northern views, such as that in the work of Pär Lagerkvist.

The relationship between art and science is an issue that has come to dominate much of the cultural climate of our time, and the book will explore aspects of Leonardo's cultural myth that facilitate explanation of how painting allied itself harmoniously and through analogical modes with his scientific investigations. This section of the book will be of interest to cognitive scientists and to anyone who wishes to explore ideas of formative mental processes as part of both cultural myth and of a continuous conception of human existence.

Among few writers to investigate Leonardo both as artist and as scientist was Paul Valéry. In two long essays on Leonardo, Valéry sought to control the antinomy between Leonardo's constructive genius and the internalizing aspect of his mind shown by the cultivation of a plastic art as a substitute for "philosophy." Two aspects of Leonardo's practice appear so far only in technical studies of his writings and drawings, and I will assert their general dominance over the output of his works: (1) with the benefit of Martin Kemp's studies of Leonardo's science, his DOUBLE PERSPECTIVE, which his own contemporaries would term illogical; and (2) his SPIROFORM conceptions, ranging from the atmospheric background of his paintings to the drawings of flying machines, birds rising in the air, swimmers, and illustrations of his wave theory. These principles, which I believe to be near the heart of Leonardo's working procedure, will also be illustrated throughout by his own writings, followed by an assessment of how these writings have moved my own hand to produce another construction of the cultural myth of Leonardo.

******

•Brief outline of contents

Preface: The Anthropology of One's Own Culture

Section 1: The Creative Powers of Leonardesque Fictions: Merezhkovsky, Freud, and Mission Painting

Section 2: Leonardo's Double Perspective

Section 3: The Androgynous Genius

•Anticipated length: ca. 200 printed pages

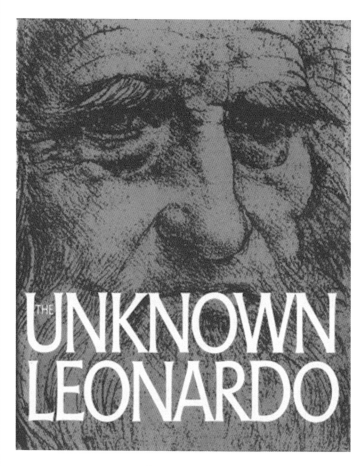

Casebound in red bookcloth with gold foil stamping; duotone offset dustjacket.

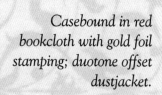

APPENDIX D

Translation by Marianne Shapiro,
"The Words of Leonardo,"
in *The Unknown Leonardo*
(New York: McGraw-Hill, 1974), pp. 293-300.

E tirato dalla mia bramosa voglia,
vago di vedere la gran copia delle varie e strane
forme fatte dalla artifiziosa natura, raggiratomi
alquanto infra gli ombrosi scogli, pervenni all'entrata di
una gran caverna, dinanzi alla quale restato
alquanto stupefatto e ignorante di tal cosa, piegato le mie reni
in arco e ferma la stanca mano sopra il ginocchio,
e colla destra mi feci tenebra
alle abbassate ... ciglia.
E spesso piegandomi in qua e in là per vedere
se dentro vi discernessi alcuna cosa e questo vietatomi
la grande oscurità che là entro era,
stato alquanto, subito salse in me 2 cose, paura
e desidèro: paura per la minacciante e scura spilonca;
desidèro per vedere se là entro fusse
alcuna miracolosa cosa.

And drawn by my ardent desire,
impatient to see the great abundance of strange forms
created by that artificer, Nature, I wandered for some time
among the shadowed rocks.
I came to the mouth of a huge cave before which I stopped
for a moment, stupefied
by such an unknown thing. I arched my back,
rested my left hand on my knee, and with my right shaded
my lowered eyes;
several times I leaned to one side, then the other,
to see if I could distinguish anything,
but the great darkness within made this impossible.
After a time there arose in me both fear and desire—
fear of the dark and menacing cave;
desire to see whether it contained
some marvelous thing.   ARUNDEL 155r

Proemio: So bene che per non essere io litterato,
che alcuno prosuntuoso gli parrà ragionevolmente
potermi biasimare coll'allegare io essere omo sanza lettere –
gente stolta!
Non sanno questi tali ch'io potrei,
sì come Mario rispose contro a' patrizi romani,
io sì rispondere dicendo: quelli che dell'altrui fatiche
sè medesimi fanno ornati le mie a me medesimo
non vogliano concedere.
Diranno che per non avere io lettere,
non potere ben dire quello di che voglio trattare.
Or non sanno questi che le mie cose son più da essere
tratte dalla sperienzia che d'altrui parola;
la quale fu maestra di chi ben scrisse, e così per maestra
la piglio e quella in tutti i casi allegherò.

Since I am not a man of letters,
I know that certain presumptuous persons will feel
justified in censuring me,
alleging that I am ignorant of writing—fools!
They do not know that I could reply, as did Marius
to the Roman nobles,
"They who adorn themselves with the labors of others will not
concede me my own."
They will hold that because of my lack of literary training
I cannot properly set forth the subjects I wish to treat.
They do not know that my subjects require for their expression
not the words of others
but experience, the mistress of all who write well.
I have taken her as my mistress
and will not cease to state it.   ATLANTICUS 119v-a

Fuggi i precetti di quelli speculatori
che le loro ragioni non sono confermate dalla isperienza.

Avoid the teachings of speculators
whose judgments are not confirmed by experience.   MS. B 4v

Se tu isplezzerai la pittura,
la quale è sola imitatrice di tutte l'opere evidenti di natura,
per certo tu sprezzerai una sottile invenzione,
la quale con filosofica e sottile speculazione
considera tutte le qualità delle forme:
aire e siti, piante, animali, erbe e fiori,
le quali son cinte d'ombra e lume;
e veramente questa è scienzia legittima figliola di natura...

If you disparage painting,
which alone imitates all the visible works of nature,
you disparage a most subtle science which by philosophical
reasoning examines all kinds of forms:
on land and in the air, plants, animals, grass, and flowers,
which are all bathed in shadow and light.
Doubtless this science
is the true daughter of nature....   MS. A 100r

Il dipintore disputa e gareggia colla natura.

The painter contends with and rivals nature.

FORSTER III 44v

Intra li studi delle naturali
considerazioni, la luce diletta più i contemplanti;
intra le cose grandi delle matematiche la certezza
della dimostrazione innalza più plecarmente

Of all studies of natural causes,
light gives greatest joy to those who consider it;
among the glories of mathematics the certainty of its
proofs most elevates the investigator's mind.

293

69

l'ingegni delli investiganti.
La prospettiva adunque è da esser preposta a tutte
le traduzioni e discipline umane, nel campo della quale la linia
radiosa complicata dà i modi delle dimostrazioni,
nella quale si truova la gloria
non tanto della matematica quanto della fisica...

Perspective, which shows how linear rays differ according
to demonstrable conditions,
should therefore be placed first among all the sciences
and disciplines of man,
for it crowns not mathematics
so much as the natural sciences....

Prospettiva è ragione dimostrativa,
per la quale la sperienzia conferma tutte le cose mandare
all'occhio per linee piramidali la lor similitudine;
e quelli corpi d'equali grandezze faranno maggiore
o minore angolo a la lor piramide secondo la varietà
della distanzia che fia da l'una a l'altra.
Linie piramidali intendo esser quelle,
le quali si partano da' superfiziali stremi de' corpi
e per distante concorso si conducano in un sol punto.
Punto dicono essere quello il quale in nessuna parte
si pò dividere,
e questo punto è quello il quale, stando ne l'occhio,
riceve in sè tutte le punte della piramide.

Perspective is the rational law by which experience
confirms that all objects transmit their image
to the eye in a pyramid of lines.
Bodies of equal size produce angles that are
more or less acute
depending on their respective distances.
I call "pyramid of lines" the lines
that emanate from the surfaces and outlines of the bodies
and, as they converge from a distance, end
in a common point.
We call a point that which cannot be divided in any way,
and that point, situated in the eye,
receives in itself the apexes of all the pyramids.

MS. A 3r

Ogni corpo empie
la circustante aria della sua similitudine,
la quale similitudine è tutta per tutto e tutta nella parte.
L'aria è piena d'infinite linie rette e radiose
insieme intersegate e intessute sanza occupazione
l'una dell'altra, [che] rappresentano a qualunque obbietto
la vera forma della lor cagione.

Every body fills the surrounding air
with images of itself, and every image appears
in its entirety and in all its parts.
The air is full of an infinity of straight lines and rays
which cut across each other without displacing each other and
which reproduce on whatever they encounter
the true form of their cause.

MS. A 2v

Perchè in tutti i casi
del moto l'acqua ha gran conformità con l'aria,
io l'allegherò per esempio alla sopraddetta proposizione.
Io dico: se tu gitterai in un medesimo tempo
2 picciole pietre alquanto distanti l'una dall'altra
sopra un pelago d'acqua sanza moto,
tu vederai causare intorno alle due predette percussioni
2 separate quantità di circuli, le quali quantità, accrescendo,
vengano a scontrarsi insieme e poi a 'ncorporarsi
intersegandosi l'un circulo coll'altro,
sempre mantenendosi per cientro i lochi
percossi dalle pietre.
E la ragion si è che benchè lì apparisca qualche
dimostrazione di movimento,
l'acqua non si parte del suo sito...
E che quel ch'io dico ti si facci più manifesto,
poni mente a quelle festuche che per lor leggerezza
stanno sopra l'acqua,
che per l'onda fatta sotto loro dall'avvenimento
de' circuli non si partan però del lor primo sito, essendo
adunque questo tal risentimento d'acqua più tosto
tremore che movimento...

I will demonstrate the proposition
that in all cases the motion of water conforms
to that of air.
If you simultaneously throw two small stones
at some distance from each other
onto a motionless body of water,
you will notice around the places of impact
two groups of widening circles
which finally meet and merge,
one circle intersecting with the other,
each having as its
center the point of impact.
The reason is
that despite some evidence of movement,
water does not leave its location....
And to ascertain the truth of what I say,
consider the reeds which by virtue of their lightness
remain above water
without being displaced by the waves
thus created under them,
for the stirring of the water is a tremor,
rather than a movement....

MS. A 61r

L'acqua percossa dall'acqua fa circuli

Water struck by water forms circles

294

dintorno al loco percosso;
per lunga distanzia la voce infra l'aria;
più lunga infra il foco;
più la mente infra l'universo;
ma perchè ell'è finita
non si astende infra lo infinito.

around the point of impact;
the voice in the air creates the same
along a greater distance; fire goes still farther,
and still farther the mind in the universe; but since
the universe is finite,
the mind does not reach infinity.

MS. H 67r

La gravità, la forza e 'l moto
accidentale insieme con la percussione son le quattro
accidentali potenzie colle quali tutte l'evidenti opere
de' mortali hanno loro essere e loro morte.

Gravity, force, and accidental motion,
together with percussion, are the four accidental
powers in which all the visible
works of mortals find their existence and their death.

FORSTER II2 116v

Ogni cosa mossa con furia seguiterà per l'aria
la linia del movimento del suo motore.
Se quello move la cosa in circulo,
s'ella fia lasciata in quel moto, il moto suo fia curvo;
e se il moto fia principiato in circulo
e finito in dirittura, in dirittura fia il suo corso;
e così sendo cominciata diritta e finita torta,
torto fia il suo cammino.
Ogni cosa mossa dal colpo si parte infra angoli uguali
del suo motore.

Every object that is hurled furiously
through the air follows its mover's line of motion.
If the object is moved and released in a circular motion,
its own motion will be curvilinear,
and if the motion began as a circle and ended as a straight
line, its course will follow a straight line, and if
its beginning was straight and its completion crooked,
its path will be tortuous.
Every object that is moved
travels at equal angles from its mover.

MS. A 81v

Ogni corpo sperico di densa e resistente superfizie,
mosso dai pari potenzia, farà tanto movimento
con sua balzi causato da duro e solio smalto quanto
a gittarlo libero per l'aria.
O mirabile giustizia di te, primo motore.
Tu non hai voluto mancare a nessuna potenzia l'ordini
e qualità de' sua necessari effetti,
con ciò sia che una potenzia debe cacciare 100 braccia
una cosa vinta da lei e quella nel suo obbedire
trova intoppo, hai ordinato che la potenzia del colpo
ricausi novo movimento, il quale per diversi balzi
recuperi la intera somma del suo debito viaggio.
E se tu misurerai la via fatta da detti balzi,
tu troverai essere di tal lunghezza qual sarebbe a trarre
con la medesima forza
una simil cosa libera per l'aria.

Every spherical body
with a dense and resistant surface,
if moved by bodies of equal force, will perform
as much movement in leaps caused by hard, solid impact
as by throwing it freely into the air.
O how wondrous is your justice, Prime Mover!
You have willed that no power lack the orders and qualities
of the acts necessary to it. Since a power must hurl
at a distance of one hundred braccia an object that
it controls, and that object obey its drive, you
ordered that the power of the blow must cause new movement,
which by diverse leaps recuperates the whole total
of its rightful journey. And if the trajectory of
those leaps is measured, it is found to be of such length
as it would take to draw a similar thing through the air
with the same force.

MS. A 24r

Ogni grave che libero discende,
al centro del mondo si dirizza; e quel che più pesa,
più presto discende;
e quanto più discende, più si fa veloce.
Tanto pesa l'acqua che si parte del suo sito per causa
della nave, quanto il peso di essa nave appunto.

Every weight that falls freely
falls toward the center of the earth;
those of greater weight fall more quickly,
and as they descend their velocity increases.
The water displaced by a ship has a weight equal
to that of the ship.

FORSTER II2 65v

Ogni moto attende al suo mantenimento
ovvero ogni corpo mosso sempre si move,
in mentre che la impressione della potenzia del suo motore
in lui si riserva.

The continuity of every motion
and the motion of every moving body
depend upon the maintenance of
power of the mover.

VOLO DEGLI UCCELLI 13 (12)r

295

Ogni piccol moto fatto dal mobile circundato dall'aria, si va mantenendo con l'impeto.

Every slightest motion performed by an object in space is maintained by its impetus.

Perchè si sostiene l'uccello sopra dell'aria. L'aria che con più velocità di mobile è percossa, con maggior somma di sè medesima si condensa. ...essendo l'aria corpo atto a condensarsi in sè medesima quando essa è percossa da moto di maggior velocità che non è quel della sua fuga, essa si prieme in sè medesima e si fa infra l'altra aria a similitudine del nuvolo... Ma quando l'uccello si trova infra 'l vento, egli pò sostenersi sopra di quello sanza battere l'alie, perchè quello offizio che fa l'alia mossa contro all'aria stando l'aria sanza moto, tal fa l'aria contro all'alia essendo quella sanza moto.

Why birds are supported in the air. Air that is struck with greatest velocity of motion condenses the most. Since air is a body capable of condensation when struck with a motion of greater velocity than its own, it then becomes as dense as a cloud.... But when the bird is in the wind, he can support himself upon it without beating his wings, for the function of wings that move against the air when it is motionless is performed by the air moving against the wings when they are motionless.

Scrivi del notare sotto l'acqua, e arai il volare dell'uccello per l'aria.

Describe underwater swimming and you will have described the flight of birds.

La scienza strumentale over machinale è nobilissima e sopra tutte l'altre utilissima, con ciò sia che mediante quella tutti li corpi animati che hanno moto fanno le loro operazioni.

Mechanical science is most noble and useful above all others, for by means of it all animated bodies in motion perform their operations.

...mia intenzione è allegare prima la sperienza e poi colla ragione dimostrare perchè tale esperienza è costretta in tal modo ad operare.

...it is my intention first to cite experience, then to demonstrate through reasoning why experience must operate in a given way.

Convertansi li elementi l'uno nell'altro, e quando l'aria si converte in acqua pel contatto ch'ell'ha colla sua fredda regione, allora essa attrae a sè con furia tutta la circunstante aria, la quale con furia si move a riempiere il loco evacuato della fuggita d'aria ...e questo è il vento.

The elements are converted into one another, and when air is converted to water by contact with its cold regions, it then furiously attracts to itself the surrounding air, which rushes to fill the vacated place... and this is the wind.

L'onda percossa nel lito per forza di vento fa il tomolo, mettendo la sua superior parte sul fondo; e per quel torna indirieto insino al loco dove di novo ripercote nella succedente onda che le viene di sotto e la rovescia indirieto con riverscio tomolo e di novo la fa ripercotere nel predetto lito; e così successivamente seguita; ora col moto superiore torna al lito e ora collo inferiore si fugge da quello.

The wave struck on its side by the wind makes a leap, moving its upper part to the bottom, and is deflected to where it beats once again upon the successive wave arising from underneath it, and reversing it, again strikes its side, and continues thus, now with motion of its upper part turning back to shore, now with inferior part turning away.

296

Ogni figura
creata dal moto, col moto si mantiene.
Quando tira vento spiana la rena, e vedi in che modo essa
crea le sue onde, e nota quanto essa si move più tarda
che 'l vento; e 'l simile fa dell'acqua
e nota le differenzie ch'è dall'acqua alla rena.

Nota il moto del livello dell'acqua,
il quale fa a uso de' capelli, che hanno due moti,
de' quali l'uno attende al peso del vello
l'altro al liniamento delle volte.
Così l'acqua ha le sue volte revertiginose,
delle quali una parte attende a l'impeto
del corso principale, l'altra attende
al moto incidente e refresso.

Scrivi come li nugoli si compongano
e come si risolvano, e che causa leva li vapori
dell'acqua dalla terra infra l'aria,
e la causa delle nebbie e dell'aria ingrossata,
e perchè si mostra più azzurra e meno azzurra una volta
che un'altra; e così scrivi le regioni dell'aria
e la causa delle nevi e delle grandini, e del ristrignersi
l'acqua e farsi dura in diaccio,
e del creare per l'aria nuove figure di neve e alli alberi
nuove figure di foglie ne' paesi freddi,
e per li sassi diacciuoli...

E già sopra a Milano, inverso Lago Maggiore,
vidi una nuvola in forma di grandissima montagna,
piena di scòli infocati, perchè li razzi del sole,
che già era all'orizzonte che rosseggiava,
la tignea del suo colore.
E questa tal nugola grande ... non si movea di suo loco;
anzi riservò nella sua sommità il lume del sole insino
a una ora e mezza di notte, tant'era la sua immensa grandezza.
E infra due ore di notte generò sì gran vento, che fu
cosa stupente, inaudita; e questo fece nel riserrarsi,
che l'aria che infra quella si rinchiudeva,
essendo premuta dalla condensazione del nugolo,
rompea e fuggia per le parte più debole, scorrendo
per l'aria con ispesso tomulto, facendo a similitudine
della spugna premuta dalla mano sotto l'acqua,
della quale l'acqua di che era imbeverata fugge infra
le dita della man che la preme,
fuggendo con impeto infra l'altr'acqua.

Come la chiarezza dell'aria nasce dall'acqua
che in quella s'è resoluta e fattasi in insensibili
graniculi, li quali, preso il lume del sole
dall'apposita parte, rendan la chiarezza che in essa aria
si dimostra; e l'azzurro che in quella apparisce nasce
dalle tenbre che dopo'essa aria si nascondano.

Every configuration of dust, smoke, and water
that is created by motion is maintained by it.
When the wind blows the sands are leveled, and you see
how it forms waves, and note how they move more slowly than
the wind; consider the waters,
and what differences exist between water and wind.

ATLANTICUS 37v-c

Observe how the movement of the surface of the water
resembles that of hair,
which has two movements,
one of which stems from the weight of the hair
and the other from its waves and curls.
In the same way, water has its turbulent curls, a part of
which follows the force of the main current, the other
obeying the movement of incidence and reflection.

WINDSOR 12579r

Show how clouds form and dissolve,
how water vapor rises from the earth into the air,
how mists form and air thickens,
and why one wave seems more blue than another;
describe the aerial regions
and the causes of snow and hail,
how water condenses
and hardens into ice,
and how new figures form in the air,
and new leaves on the trees,
and icicles on the stones of cold places....

MS. F 35r

And recently above Milan toward Lake Maggiore,
I saw a cloud in the shape of an immense mountain
covered with fiery stones,
for it was tinged with red
by the sun on the horizon.
This huge cloud... stood motionless;
such was its immensity that its summit contained
the sun's light for one hour and a half into night.
And within two hours of night
it produced so great a wind,
it was a stupefying, unheard-of thing;
the air contained in it, compressed by condensation,
erupted and escaped through the cloud's weakest part,
rushing tumultuously, as happens
when a sponge is pressed under water by a hand
and the water it had absorbed
escapes between the fingers of the hand
and through the surrounding water.

LEICESTER 28r

The clarity of air derives from water
dissolved into imperceptible drops
which take the sunlight from the opposite direction,
thereby rendering the air clear;
and the blue that appears in the air is caused
by the shadows concealed in it.

LEICESTER 20r

297

Movesi l'aria come fiume e tira con seco di nuvoli,
sì come l'acqua corrente
tira tutte le cose che sopra di lei si sostengano.

The air moves like a river
and draws clouds in its wake, just as rushing water
draws with it all things that are above its surface. MS. G 10r

La fiamma fa moto infra l'aria
quale fa l'aria infra l'acqua cioè moto fressuoso;
e massime dov'è gran fiamma.

Flame moves in the air as air moves in water,
in a flexible motion,
especially from where the flame is great. ARUNDEL 139v

Quando il sole s'innalza e caccia le nebbie
e si comincia a rischiarare e colli,
da quella parte donde esse si partano e' fansi azzurri
e fumano inverso le nebbie fuggenti...

When the sun rises
and drives away the mist,
the hills become blue where the mist is departing
and smoke in the direction of the escaping mist.... ARUNDEL 169r

Noterai nel tuo ritrarre come infra le ombre
sono ombre insensibili d'oscurità e di figura...
Le cose vedute infra 'l lume e l'ombre si dimosterranno
di maggiore rilievo che quelle che son
nel lume o nell'ombre.

You will observe in your painting
that shadows among shadows
are imperceptible in density and outline....
Things seen between light and shadow will display
much more relief than those seen in light or in shadow. MS. E 17r

Poni mente per le strade, sul fare della sera,
i volti d'omini e donne, quando è cattivo tempo,
quanta grazia e dolcezza si vede in loro.

Observe how much grace and sweetness
are to be seen in the faces of men and women on the streets,
with the approach of evening in bad weather. MS. A 100v

Questi libri
contengano in ne' primi della natura
dell'acqua in sé e ne' sua moti;
li altri contengano delle cose fatte da e sua corsi,
che mutano il mondo di centro e di figura.

These books contain
the nature of water and its motion;
the others contain the things produced by its flow
which have changed the face
and the center of the world. LEICESTER 5r

Io truovo il sito della terra
essere ab antico nelle sue pianure tutto occupato
e coperto dall'acque salse; e i monti, ossa della terra,
con le loro larghe base, penetrare e elevarsi infra l'aria,
coperti e vestiti di molta e alta terra.
Di poi le molte piogge, accrescimento de' fiumi,
con ispessi lavamenti ha dispogliato in parte l'alte cime
d'essi monti, lasciando in loco della terra il sasso...
E la terra delle spiagge e dell'alte cime
delle montagne è già discesa alle sue base e ha alzato
i fondi de' mari ch'esse basi circavano
e fatta discoperta pianura, e di lì in alcun loco,
per lontano spazio, ha cacciato i mari.

I conclude that in oldest times
salt waters entirely occupied and covered the earth,
and the mountains,
skeleton of the earth with their wide bases,
penetrated and arose into the air,
covered and decked with abundant, deep soil.
Since then great rains, enlarging the streams,
despoiled with their frequent lavings the high peaks
of those mountains, leaving stone in place of soil....
And the earth of the beaches and of high mountain peaks
has already descended to their bases and raised the
sea bottom which they had surrounded, and uncovered a plain,
from which in some places it has driven the seas. ATLANTICUS 126v-b

Nessuna parte della terra
si scopre dalla consumazione del corso dell'acqua,
che già non fussi superfizie di terra
veduta dal sole.

No part of the earth exposes itself
by the depredations of the course of the waters
which was not once a land surface
seen by the sun. ATLANTICUS 45v-a

L'acqua disfa li monti e riempie le valle
e vorrebbe ridurre la terra in perfetta spericità,
s'ella potessi.

The waters destroy the mountains, fill the valleys,
and would reduce the world to perfect sphericalness
if they could.   ATLANTICUS 185v-c

Perpetui son li bassi lochi
del fondo del mare e il contrario son le cime dei monti;
seguita che la terra si farà sperica e tutta coperta
dall'acque e sarà inabitabile.

The depths of the sea bottom are perpetual,
and the peaks of the mountains are not;
it follows that the earth will become spherical,
covered with water, and uninhabitable.   MS. F 52r

Farai regola e misura di ciascun muscolo
e renderai ragione di tutti li loro uffizi e in che modo
s'adoprano e chi li move.

You will take the measure of all the muscles
and learn their functions,
who moves them, and how they are implemented.   ANAT. B 27r

E questo vecchio, di poche ore inanzi la sua morte,
mi disse lui passare cento anni
e che non si sentiva alcun mancamento nella persona,
altro che debolezza;
e così standosi a sedere sopra uno letto
nello spedale di Santa Maria Nova di Firenze,
senza altro movimento o segno d'alcuno accidente,
passò di questa vita.
E io ne feci notomia,
per vedere la causa di sì dolce morte:
la quale trovai venire meno per mancamento di
sangue e arteria, che notria il core
e li altri membri inferiori,
li quali trovai molti aridi, stenuati e secchi.
La qual notomia discrissi assai diligentemente
e con gran facilità, per essere privato
di grasso e di omore,
che assai impedisce la cognizione delle parte...

And an old man,
only a few hours before he died,
told me that he had lived for one hundred years
without experiencing any
physical failure other than weakness;
and sitting on the bed in the hospital
of Santa Maria Nova in Florence,
he passed from this life,
giving no sign of any accident.
And I dissected his body,
in order to understand the cause of so easy a death.
I discovered that it came to him
through a lack of blood
in the arteries that fed the heart and the lower parts,
which were used up and dried out.
I performed this dissection
minutely and easily, as there were neither fat nor humors
to impede recognition of anatomical parts....   ANAT. B10v

Tu non farai mai se non confusione
nella dimostrazione dei muscoli e lor siti,
nascimenti e fini, se prima non fai una dimostrazione
di muscoli sottili a uso di fila di refe;
e così li potrai figurare l'un sopra dell'altro
come li ha situati la natura...

You will only confuse
your representation of the muscles and their location,
derivation, and purpose if you first
do not show the network of the small muscles;
depict them one above the other
as nature has placed them....   ANAT. A 18r

E tu che di' esser meglio
il vedere fare la notomia che vedere tali disegni,
diresti bene se fussi possibile
veder tutte queste cose,
che in tali disegni si dimostrano, in una sola figura;
nella quale, con tutto il tuo ingegno,
non vedrai e non arai notizia se non d'alquante
poche vene; delle quali io,
per averne vera e piena notizia,
ho disfatti più di dieci corpi umani,
destruggendo ogni altri membri,
consumando con minutissime particule tutta la carne

You who claim that it is better
to watch an anatomical demonstration
than to look at these drawings–you would be right,
if you could see in a single form
all the details shown in the drawings;
with all your ability,
you would not see or get to know in one form
more than a few veins.
To obtain an exact and complete knowledge,
I have dissected more than ten human bodies,
destroying all the other parts
and removing to the last particle

299

che dintorno a esse vene si trovava,
sanza insanguinarle,
se non d'insensibile insanguinamento delle vene capillare.
E un sol corpo non bastava a tanto tempo;
che bisognava procedere di mano in mano
in tanti corpi, che si finissi la intera cognizione;
la qual ripricai due volte per vedere le differenzie.
E se tu arai l'amore di tal cosa,
tu sarai forse impedito dallo stomaco;
e se questo non ti impedisce, tu sarai forse impedito
dalla paura coll'abitare nelli tempi notturni
in compagnia di tali morti,
squartati e scorticati e spaventevoli a vederli;
e se questo non t'impedisce,
forse ti mancherà il disegno bono,
il qual s'appartiene a tal figurazione.
E se tu arai il disegno,
e' non sarà accompagnato dalla prospettiva;
e se sarà accompagnato, e' ti mancherà l'ordine delle
dimostrazion geometriche e l'ordine delle calculazion
delle forze e valimento de'muscoli;
o forse ti mancherà la pazienzia, se tu non sarai diligente.
Delle quali, se in me tutte queste cose sono state o no,
centoventi libri da me composti
ne daran sentenzia del si o del no,
nelli quali non sono stato impedito nè d'avarizia
o negligenzia, ma sol dal tempo. Vale.

all the flesh surrounding these veins,
without any bleeding other than that,
nearly imperceptible, of the capillary veins.
A single body did not suffice for so long a time;
I had to proceed by stages with many bodies
to achieve complete knowledge.
I did this twice in order to understand the differences.
In spite of your love of such investigations,
you may be deterred by repugnance;
if not, then by the fear of spending the nights
in the company of corpses that are cut up
and flayed and horrible to look upon.
And if this does not deter you,
then perhaps you lack the skill in drawing
necessary for such representations;
and if you can draw,
you may have no knowledge of perspective;
and if you have it,
you may not be versed in geometrical exposition
or in the method of calculating
the forces and energy of the muscles;
or perhaps you are lacking in patience,
so that you will not be diligent.
Whether or not I possess all these qualities
will be attested in one hundred twenty books,
whose composition was delayed not by avarice or negligence,
but by time alone. Farewell.   ANAT. C 13v

Se guarderai le stelle sanza razzi
(come si fa vederle per un piccolo foro
fatto colla strema punta de la sottile acucchia,
e quel posto quasi a toccare l'occhio), tu vedrai esse
stelle essere tanto minime,
che nulla cosa pare essere minore.
E veramente la lunga distanzia dà loro ragionevole
diminuizione, ancora che molte vi sono,
che son moltissime volte maggiore che la stella
ch'è la terra coll'acqua.
Ora pensa quel che parrebbe quessa nostra stella
in tanta distanzia, e considera poi quante stelle
si metterebbe' e per longitudine e latitudine infra
esse stelle, le quali sono
seminate per esso spazio tenebroso.

If you scrutinize the stars without rays
(as is done through a little hole
in the end of a small lens, placed
so as almost to touch the eye),
you will perceive these stars
as so tiny that nothing could be smaller.
And indeed,
the great distance confers upon them a certain diminution,
though many of them are several times larger
than that star which is our earth and its waters.
Now consider
what our star would seem at such a distance,
and how many stars could be longitudinally
and latitudinally interposed
between those which are scattered through dark space.   MS. F 5r

Alli ambiziosi,
che non si contentano del benefizio della vita
nè della bellezza del mondo,
è dato per penitenzia che lor medesimi strazino essa vita,
e che non possegghino la utilità e bellezza del mondo.

The ambitious, who are not content
with the gifts of life and the beauty of the world,
are given the penitence of ruining
their own lives and never possessing the utility
and beauty of the world.   ATLANTICUS 91v-a

O speculatore delle cose,
non ti laldare di conoscere le cose che ordinariamente
per sè medesima la natura conduce,
ma rallegrati di conoscere il fine di quelle cose
che son disegnate dalla mente tua.

O investigator,
do not flatter yourself that you know
the things nature performs for herself,
but rejoice in knowing the purpose
of those things designed by your own mind.

MS. G 47r

This book was typeset in Goudy Oldstyle,
designed by Fred Goudy in 1915 for the
American Type Foundry,
and inspired by a portrait by Hans Holbein the Younger.

Made in the USA
Charleston, SC
19 December 2012